Making Sense of Media and Politics

Politics is above all a contest, and the news media are the central arena for viewing that competition. Political coverage does not occur in a vacuum, however. One of the central concerns of political communication has to do with the myriad ways in which politics has an impact on the news media and the equally diverse ways in which the media influences politics. Both of these aspects in turn weigh heavily on the effects such political communication has on mass citizens.

In *Making Sense of Media and Politics*, Gadi Wolfsfeld introduces readers to the most important concepts that serve as a framework for examining the interrelationship of media and politics:

- Political power can usually be translated into power over the news media.
- When authorities lose control over the political environment they also lose control over the news.
- There is no such thing as objective journalism (nor can there be).
- The media is dedicated more than anything else to telling a good story.
- The most important effects of the news media on citizens tend to be unintentional and unnoticed.

By identifying these five key principles of political communication, the author examines those who package and send political messages, those who transform political messages into news, and the effect all this has on citizens. The result is a brief, engaging guide to help make sense of the wider world of media and politics and an essential companion to more in-depths studies of the field.

Gadi Wolfsfeld is Full Professor in the departments of political science and communication at the Hebrew University of Jerusalem. He also holds the Danny Arnold Chair in Communication. He is former chair of the political communication section of the American Political Science Association. Dr. Wolfsfeld is the author of *Media and the Path to Peace* and *Media and Political Conflict: News from the Middle East*, as well as co-editor (together with Philippe Maarek) of *Political Communication in a New Era: A Cross-National Perspective*.

Making Sense of Media and Politics

Five Principles in Political Communication

Gadi Wolfsfeld

Routledge
Taylor & Francis Group

NEW YORK AND LONDON

First published 2011
by Routledge
270 Madison Avenue, New York, NY 10016

Simultaneously published in the UK
by Routledge
2 Park Square, Milton Park, Abingdon, Oxon OX14 4RN

Routledge is an imprint of the Taylor & Francis Group, an informa business

Typeset in Garamond by EvS Communication Networx, Inc.
Printed and bound in the United States of America on acid-free paper
by Walsworth Publishing Company, Marceline, MO

Library of Congress Cataloging in Publication Data
Wolfsfeld, Gadi.
Making sense of media and politics : five principles in political communication / Gadi Wolfsfeld.
p. cm.
Includes bibliographical references.
1. Communication in politics. 2. Mass media—Political aspects. 3. Press and politics. I. Title.
JA85.W65 2011
320.01'4—dc22
2010040006

ISBN13: 978-0-415-88522-5 (hbk)
ISBN13: 978-0-415-88523-2 (pbk)
ISBN13: 978-0-203-83987-4 (ebk)

This book is dedicated to my family:
Lauren, Dana, Noa and Eli.
They are and will always be the most important reason for everything.

Table of Contents

Acknowledgements

It was about thirty-five years ago that I was introduced the fascinating world of political communication. It all started with a class I took as a graduate student in the department of political science at M.I.T. The person who taught that class would eventually become my thesis advisor: Ithiel de Sola Pool. Ithiel, who has since passed away, was an inspiration and mentor to countless students including myself. He was also not only one of the first political scientists to study the ongoing interactions between politics and media but a path breaker in thinking about the impact of changing communication technology on society. I owe him a great debt for both pointing me in the right direction and for providing me with the analytical and methodological tools that have served me so well for so long.

My next debt is by far my greatest: to my wife. Lauren and I have been married for over thirty years and (as many of our friends continually point out) she was the best thing that ever happened to me. She has endured with grace many years of my complaints, frustrations, and whining and only some that annoying behavior comes from writing this book. Among her many other talents Lauren has always been my first editor. One of the primary advantages of having her read the first drafts is that I am much less likely to embarrass myself. Lauren has read every sentence in this book and her instincts about what works and what doesn't are always an essential element in the writing process. The fact that she also keeps me (mostly) sane is also a major help and I am eternally grateful for that as well.

I also want to thank friends and colleagues who read and commented on earlier drafts. I am especially grateful to those who took a significant amount of time from their own research and writing to read the entire manuscript: Sean Aday, Eitan Alimi, Scott Althaus, Hadas Eyal, and Tamir Sheafer. A number of other colleagues also contributed to the final product by agreeing to my (always) urgent requests to read particular sections: Bob Entman, Doris Graber, Abby Jones, Judy Rudy, Shaul Shenhav, Yariv Tsfati, David Weiner, and Moran Yarchi. Avner de-Shalit came up with the first part of this book's title and I thank him for the great idea. I would also like to thank the anonymous reviewers from Routledge who provided extremely important and detailed critiques of the manuscript. I also want to acknowledge Mary Altman the editorial assistant at Routledge who was always extremely gracious, diligent, and efficient in dealing with the dozens of administrative details that arose trying to get the manuscript in shape and delivered on time. Finally I want to thank my editor at Routledge, Michael Kerns, who was always encouraging and helpful throughout the entire process. I am always tempted at this juncture to attribute any faults, mistakes, or weaknesses in this book to all those who helped me. I have to be honest however and to take any blame completely on myself.

Introduction

Politics is above all a contest. It is a contest between Republicans and Democrats, between Pro-Life and Pro-Choice activists, between the United States and Iran, between candidates running for mayor, between conservatives and progressives, between oppressed people and their oppressors, and between a large variety of other actors all trying to defeat their rivals. The news media are an extremely important part of almost every political contest; they provide an audience of thousands, tens of thousands, or even millions of people. The nature of what we call the "media" may have changed considerably after the creation of the Internet, but the need to be heard remains a central part of the political game. All political actors want to have their messages sent to as large an audience as possible in order to mobilize supporters to their cause. It is only a slight exaggeration to say that if you don't exist in the media, you don't exist politically.

The goal of this book is to propose five basic principles you should know concerning politics and the news media. I certainly hope you will learn a lot more than five things when you're finished. But if you only remember the five principles, you will be ahead of the game in understanding how these two worlds come together. These five principles will also give you a framework for understanding many more elements of political communication. Hopefully, the next time you look at the news or think about politics you will see them in a whole new light.

The book is intended to be brief and is divided into three sections. The first section (Chapters 1 and 2) looks at the issue from the political actors' perspective. These are the politicians and other activists who are constantly competing over the news media in order to send their messages. The second section (Chapters 3 and 4) examines the media's viewpoint by dealing with how journalists turn political information into news. The media pursue their own interests when they construct the news; sometimes these goals complement what political actors are trying to achieve, but at other times the press can make leaders' lives downright miserable. The final section (Chapter 5) looks at those who consume the news: the public. Research in this field deals with what is known as media *effects*. The important questions have to do with the different types of impact the media can have on people and which citizens are the most likely to be influenced.

Thus the three sections examine those who package and send political messages, those who transform political messages into news, and the effect all this has on ordinary citizens. The order of these sections is anything but random. One of the major themes of this book is that to understand the role the media play in politics, you have to always *start* by looking at the political context in which the news media are operating. Every journalist constructs news stories that are firmly rooted in a particular time, place, culture, and set of political circumstances. In addition, journalists almost always react to political events rather than initiate them. The news media do play an essential role in all this but anyone who hopes to understand the full picture should always begin by thinking systematically about politics.

Here is the basic structure of the book.

Section I: Political Actors Compete Over the News Media

Chapter 1: Political Power and Power Over the Media

The first principle goes like this: *Political power can usually be translated into power over the news media.* One of the most enduring lessons in the field of political communication is that those who have political power not only find it much easier to get coverage, but also are in a much better position to get their messages across. The news media are more interested in elites, and this preference has far reaching consequences for the role the media play in politics. A good deal of this chapter will focus on the competition between governments and their opponents because the ability of weaker adversaries to be heard is a central component of any healthy democracy.

Those without political power find themselves in a very difficult position with regard to the news media. Due to definitions of what is considered news, weaker challengers often have the choice of either doing something outrageous or being banished to that distant land known as obscurity. The harsh rules that determine who is denied access not only influence the fate of oppositional political parties and movements, they also affect the ability of weaker countries to be effective on the world stage. In general one can say that in many areas, when it comes to media attention, the rich get richer and the poor remain poor.

There are some who feel that in the digital age political power has become less important in determining influence over the media. When anybody with a video phone can become a journalist and political movements can simply load their messages on YouTube, who cares about getting on the evening news? But even in the digital age, it turns out, the politically powerful still have quite a few tricks for staying on top. The question of how much technology has reduced the gap between the politically powerful and the weak will receive a fair amount of attention in this first chapter.

Chapter 2: Political Control and Media Independence

Here is the second principle you need to know about media and politics: *When the authorities lose control over the political environment they also lose control over the news.* Despite the fact that those in charge have significant advantages over their opponents, they rarely have complete and ongoing power over the media. Think, for example, about what happened to the coverage of President George W. Bush in the aftermath of hurricane Katrina that did so much damage to New Orleans. The majority of journalists and citizens came to the conclusion that the administration relief efforts were inadequate and this was certainly reflected in the press coverage.[1] The same can be said about the administration's seeming lack of control over the economy during the major recession that began in December of 2007.

The best way to understand what happens in these situations is to look at the extent to which those in charge have control over what is called the "political environment." The political environment refers to everything people are doing, thinking, and saying about an issue at a particular place and time. A helpful way to think about this is to break down the political environment surrounding an issue into three components: the authorities' level of control over events, their control over the flow of relevant information, and their ability to maintain a high level of elite consensus surrounding their policies. When you examine any issue using these three factors you gain a much better understanding of how the powerful can become weaker, and how the weak can become powerful.

As further detailed in Chapter 2, it is especially revealing to look at how this principle can be used to explain the varying roles of the news media in wars and attempts to make peace. One of the more intriguing examples concerning peace processes is to look at the very different role the news media played in attempts to bring an end to the conflict in Northern Ireland and compare it to similar attempts that were made in the Middle East. The news media provided an important source of support for peace in Northern Ireland but were serious obstacles in attempts to bring a peace agreement between Israel and the Palestinians. Here too, the key to understanding this difference is the ability of leaders to maintain political control.

There is good reason to believe that the "new" media have made it more difficult for all leaders to maintain control over the political environment, especially concerning the free flow of information. It is especially intriguing to ask how news of wars has changed in the digital age.

Section II: Turning Politics Into News

In the second section of the book, the discussion moves from the actors' perspectives to those of the journalists. As noted earlier, the news media have their own interests and goals and this section explains how those preferences shape the news.

Chapter 3: No Such Thing as Objective News

The third principle goes like this: *There is no such thing as objective journalism (nor can there be).* If there is one thing everyone seems to know about the news, it's that it is biased. Most of the complaining comes from members of the right wing who refer to journalists as bleeding heart liberals—and that's the *nicest* thing they have to say about them. There are also, though, quite a few people on the Left who say the news media are too nationalistic and tied to corporate interests. The issue, as usual, is far more complicated than most people think. True objectivity is totally impossible. The very fact that journalists have to choose to report on just a few items among a ridiculously large number of world events tells you that, even in the digital age, journalists have to make subjective judgments about what people need to know and what can be ignored. There are also far more important types of news bias that most people don't even recognize and these too are discussed in detail in Chapter 3.

A good deal of this chapter deals with the notion of *news frames*. News frames are organizing devices journalists use to tell a coherent story ("The War on Terror"). When political actors compete over the news media, they also have their own frames they are trying to promote. When the news media exhibit a preference for one frame instead of another, it can provide significant advantages to certain antagonists. Take, for example, the U.S. debate concerning the war in Iraq. At one point in the debate, the Bush administration was attempting to promote a "Stay the Course" frame that argued for the importance of continuing the war effort until the fighting could be turned over to Iraqi troops. Critics of the war, on the other hand, used a "Futile War" frame that talked about the need to withdrawal American troops as soon as possible. As you can imagine, understanding how journalists decide which news frame to use can be extremely helpful in understanding how such political contests play out.

Chapter 4: Telling a Good Story

The fourth principle reads as follows: *The media are dedicated more than anything else to telling a good story and this can often have a major impact on the political process.* Those who have been around for a while have noticed that journalists seem to be increasingly concerned with grabbing our attention rather than providing us with intelligent coverage ("Toddler Drives Eighteen-wheeler to Grandma's House: Details at 11"). The term often used to describe this trend is: infotainment. The idea is that this type of news is not really pure information and or just entertainment; it is something in between. It turns out that because most news media put such a premium on drama it has an effect on both how political actors behave and how the public sees politics. This emphasis on drama is another important example of how the news media transform the world of politics into something new.

This is also one of the reasons the political news is so negative and cynical. There is nothing newsworthy about a senator doing a good job. A senator who is having an affair on the other hand, is considered news especially if reporters can get a good picture of the lover. Speaking of cynicism, the infotainment world is not only about news it also includes late-night talk shows and shows like *The Daily Show* or *The Colbert Report*. Political ridicule has become a big business throughout the world, and this too has a way of transforming how people think about politics. There are many who believe that this incessant flow of cynical political news and entertainment leads to a general decline in public trust. This question is also discussed in Chapter 4.

The media's obsession with drama has perhaps its most profound influence when it comes to how they cover terrorism and war. One claim is that the contest over audience share provides terrorist groups with a disproportionate amount of media attention which furthers their cause. Many terrorist leaders have been turned into bona fide celebrities with the international news media anxiously waiting for their latest press release. Equally important, the news media are extremely efficient tools for mobilizing people to go to war, but are much less useful in attempts to bring peace.

Chapter 5: The Media Get You When You're Not Paying Attention

The final principle reads: *The most important effects of the news media on citizens tend to be unintentional and unnoticed.* Those who study effects are interested in how and how much the news media influence the way people think, feel, and behave. The truth is that this has been a controversial topic for as long as anybody can remember. The reason for the fascination should be fairly obvious. When it comes right down to it, what we really want to predict is how much the news media affects things like public opinion, political tolerance, political participation, violence, and voting. After all, if the news doesn't really have an effect on people then why bother studying it?

When it comes to the news, many of the most important effects are unintended by journalists and unnoticed by their audience. The effects are unintentional because, contrary to popular opinion, journalists do not spend most of their time attempting to sway public opinion. There are, of course, exceptions, especially in the area of investigative journalism, but the primary motivation of the vast majority of news professionals is to produce good stories; any effects that occur because of those stories should be seen as unintentional byproducts.

The most important influences of the media are also *unnoticed* in that citizens are usually not aware they are being influenced. Most people are pretty good at defending themselves when they realize somebody is trying to persuade them, but they are more susceptible when they're not paying attention. Take, for example, the fact that the American news media has so few news stories about Africa. This means that despite the fact that millions of people are dying in Africa from disease and wars, few Americans are going to think about that topic when they go to the ballot box. It's not that either journalists or the public have anything *against* Africa, it's simply that these stories are almost never considered interesting enough to be covered in the news.

A Few Cautionary Warnings before Starting the Trip

Many authors who publish this type of book state their case with a remarkable amount of certainty. This is especially true about non-fiction best sellers. They are written as if there are no exceptions, no counter-arguments, and no conditions; everything works perfectly. In some ways it's similar to what happens in the news: you have to overstate your case if you want people to pay attention.

Social scientists however are not really certain about anything (that's one of the reasons we make lousy news commentators). We've been taught from an early age to doubt *everything*, even (or especially) what we write. That's why you will find us constantly using terms like: "generally," "often," "likely," "in most cases," and "it would seem." So please read this book critically and if there are some parts you disagree with, you may very well be right.

There's also another tradition social scientists have when they are writing. We tend to apologize in advance for all the things that have been left out of the discussion. This is a preemptive strike on all our critics who are going to complain about what's missing. It's similar to what happens when defense attorneys ask their own witnesses a long list of denigrating questions in order to take away some of the prosecution's weapons (or at least that's what they do on television).

There are two major topics that receive insufficient attention in the book. The first is that a good deal of time is spent talking about "the news media" as if all media were the same. While there is quite a bit of discussion about possible differences between the traditional and new media, there is almost no discussion about the differences between television, radio, and newspapers or about the distinction between national and local news. These are important differences, but you won't find much about that topic here.

The second major omission has to do with the economics of news. Much has been written about how much of what happens in the news business is determined by economic factors. To give just one example, there is an increasing concern that newspapers will soon become extinct because so many people are turning to the Internet as their primary source for information. If this prediction comes to pass, it could lead to an entirely different form of communication between leaders and the public. While there are several references to these types of issues in the book, there is not enough here for those who are especially interested in this perspective.

A different type of warning to readers concerns the fact that most of the examples that are used come from the United States. One excuse for this ethnocentric perspective is that most of the researchers who work in the field of political communication are Americans. The book does contain, it is true, more than the usual number of examples from Israel and Northern Ireland because that is where I did a good deal of my research. Nevertheless, not all of the ideas that are developed here are applicable to other countries. The most glaring example has to do with the lack of attention given to the role of the news media in non-democratic countries. That's a whole different kettle of fish. It is not at all clear how many of the ideas developed here can be used when one is talking about places where journalists have little editorial discretion. So keep that in mind as well.

I hope that despite all these cautions, reservations, and warnings, you'll enjoy the journey.

Section I

Political Actors Compete Over the News Media

This is where it all starts. Political actors all trying to have an impact: on their communities, on their country, and on the world. They come in all shapes and forms. Some are powerful others are weak. Some have radical new ideas involving serious change while others prefer either the status quo or some minor reforms. There are political leaders, political parties, political movements, commercial companies, interest groups, lobbies, trade unions, neighborhood groups, terrorist groups, and sometimes just a few individuals who get together because they're angry about something.

One of the most important things all of these groups share is that at one point or another they want the news media to help them achieve their goals. Getting coverage, especially positive coverage, can bring lots of benefits. Take for example what media coverage can do for political movements. Sympathetic coverage in some instances can bring new members and supporters, help them raise money, raise their issues onto the public agenda, allow them to form political alliances and put pressure on political leaders. Many times publicity doesn't bring a group anything more than a nice feeling that one's name is in the newspaper. But in terms of potential, it is hard to think of many assets that can do so much for a political actor as gaining regular access to the news media.

One of the major problems confronting all political actors is that they must compete with hundreds and sometimes thousands of other actors who also want to get into the news. It is a difficult competition especially for those without any political standing. The first two chapters are designed to provide you with the basic rules of this competition. Chapter 1 deals with one of the most important rules: the greater an actor's political power, the more likely they are to get into the news. This one rule, it turns out, has tremendously important ramifications for not only how the political world is covered, but also on politics. Chapter 2 deals with ways in which the powerful, despite these advantages, can lose power over the new media.

1 Political Power and Power Over the Media

Power has made Reality its Bitch

—*Mark Danner*[1]

Think about two political actors, each trying to get into the news. For now let's talk only about the traditional news media (the new media will come into play a bit later). Assume, for the sake of argument that both are from the same political party, both have similar political views, and both look equally good in front of the camera. But there's one small difference between them: one is the president of the United States and the other is a new congressman from North Dakota. Presidents have a huge number of journalists assigned to them and can appear in the news any time they want. The congressman, on the other hand, has to compete with a horde of other politicians and convince reporters that he has something newsworthy to say. The president never has any problem getting into the national news, while the new congressman will be lucky if he gets covered in the local news.

Other powerful people in the government, whether it be the U.S. secretary of state, the secretary of defense, or the Speaker of the House also have little trouble getting into the news. If we were to build a ladder of influence from the most powerful people in Washington to the least important, we would have a pretty accurate measure of their chance of getting into the national news. Here's a good illustration of how political power leads to power over the media. Anybody who is reading this book probably knows the name of the secretary of state. Now try to name the secretary of Veterans Affairs. Unless you have some reason to be concerned with veteran issues, chances are you have no idea.

The reason, of course, is that the secretary of Veterans Affairs is simply not considered newsworthy, unless (s)he gets in trouble. A good rule of thumb is that journalists run after the politically powerful and politically weak run after journalists. This brings us to the first of the five principles. *Political power can usually be translated into power over the news media.*

One reason journalists consider the powerful more newsworthy is that these are the people who are most likely to have an impact on the country and the world. The president, after all, can go to war. The chance that an individual member of Congress can have a major impact on the political process is slim unless they are the deciding vote in an important piece of legislation. Even then, their fame is likely to be brief and they will quickly return to obscurity.

Here's another way to think of this idea. The relationship between journalists and political leaders can be considered a *competitive symbiosis*. It is a symbiotic relationship because each depends on the other in order to achieve their goals. Leaders want publicity and the journalists want interesting information they can turn into news. The reason the relationship is also competitive is that each wants to get the most from the other while "paying" as little as possible. Leaders want to get lots of publicity without having to reveal too much and reporters want to get the juiciest information without having to give a free ride to the politician. The more powerful leaders have the best information to "sell" and that's why journalists compete for the privilege of getting it, especially if they can get first crack at the story.

The fact that political power can be translated into power over the news media does not mean that the weaker political actors never get into the news. The news media have a preference for conflicts that is just as important as their preference for power. There is also an expectation that journalists will attempt to maintain a certain balance in news coverage. This means that even if they give a great deal of coverage to a presidential speech they will then allow the opposition to respond. Many talk shows also encourage a lively debate because that always makes the show more appealing.

Nevertheless, there is still something inherently elitist about these debates. Political movements and groups outside of the Washington Beltway are rarely invited to participate. So the journalists' notion of balance really means finding a balance between Republican and Democratic leaders. Political scientist Lance Bennett has done extremely important work on this issue and he argues that the best way to understand this is to think of this process as a form of "indexing."[2] The news media mostly focus on what these elites are saying and doing and they record it. If neither the government nor the opposition is talking about an issue, even an important issue, the news media will likewise, simply ignore it. Equally important, claims Bennett, this obsession with elites also severely limits the *range* of opinions that are talked about in the news media. Researcher Jonanthan Mermin makes a similar point suggesting that the news media often seem to serve as "transcribers of official utterances."[3]

This reluctance of the press to express any independent opinion about issues can have serious consequences for public debates about issues. A useful example has to do with the public debate over the Iraq War. The major argument for going to war was the firm belief in Washington that Saddam Hussein had developed Weapons of Mass Destruction (WMD). Within a relatively short amount of time, it became clear that this was not the case, yet public support for the war remained surprisingly high.

Research on this topic suggests one of the reasons was the lack of much critical coverage in the press. In a book entitled *Why the Press Failed* Lance Bennett,

Regina Lawrence, and Steven Livingston attempted to explain this anomaly.[4] One of the more important explanations was that the Democratic leadership in Congress and the Senate was extremely uncomfortable criticizing the president about the war until much later in the conflict. There were plenty of critics outside of Washington, but the media's overdependence on elite opinion apparently prevented them from providing the American public with an alternative perspective.

Mermin has a wonderful quote by TV journalist Jim Lehrer that provides a telling demonstration of this point with regard to the war in Iraq:

> The word occupation ... was never mentioned in the run-up to the war. It was liberation. This was [talked about in Washington as] a war of liberation, not a war of occupation. So as a consequence, those of us in journalism never even looked at the issue of occupation.[5]

In other words, unless the political leadership is debating an issue, journalists are rarely able to bring other perspectives to the table. Some might argue that this is how representative democracy should work. These are after all the people who were elected to lead. True democracies however must have a genuinely independent press who present a wide range of viewpoints for us to consider.

Power Comes in Many Forms

The idea that power leads to media access is not limited to politicians. There are also individuals, organizations, and companies that are inherently newsworthy because, among other reasons, they have vast resources that also allow them to have a major impact on society. When Microsoft or Google speak about political issues that affect their industry, the news media listen. The same is true about political organizations and even protest movements. An organization the size of Greenpeace—which has offices in over forty countries—may not have the type of access afforded a major U.S. cabinet member, but they are much more likely to get reporters to their events than a small local group of environmentalists protesting against a factory accused of polluting their water.

The fact that power translates into access to the news media can also be applied to cities, states, and even countries. One is much more likely to hear news that comes from the richest and more populated states (e.g., New York, California) than from the poorer states (e.g., Arkansas). And people living in Europe are more likely to hear what is happening in the United States than anything happening in Africa. It is sad but true that Europeans are more likely to know what is happening with Paris Hilton, Britney Spears, and the late Michael Jackson than about political leaders in Nigeria. One of the most important rules of international news is that there is always a flood of information that flows from the haves to the have-nots and a mere trickle that runs in the opposite direction.

Not Just More Coverage But Usually More Positive

Does the fact that powerful elites get covered *more* mean that they get covered more positively? The answer, for the most part, is yes. There are basically two doors for getting into the news. The front door is reserved for VIPs: the people with political power. When these people enter, they are usually treated with respect. They are covered because of who they are as much as for what they are doing or saying. Here is a typical front door story from the *New York Times* that appeared in September 2009.

White House Scraps Bush's Approach to Missile Shield

WASHINGTON — President Obama scrapped his predecessor's proposed antiballistic missile shield in Eastern Europe on Thursday and ordered instead the development of a reconfigured system designed to shoot down short- and medium-range Iranian missiles. In one of the biggest national security reversals of his young presidency, Mr. Obama canceled former President George W. Bush's plan to station a radar facility in the Czech Republic and 10 ground-based interceptors in Poland. Instead, he plans to deploy smaller SM-3 interceptors by 2011, first aboard ships and later in Europe, possibly even in Poland or the Czech Republic. Mr. Obama said that the new system "will provide stronger, smarter and swifter defenses of American forces and America's allies" to meet a changing threat from Iran.[6]

In these types of stories political leaders are basically using the press as an electronic bulletin board. They announce what they are going to do and provide carefully prepared explanations about why they are doing it. Now this doesn't mean that every new organ will be equally accommodating. Thus the Fox News story for the same day covered the announcement much more negatively.[7] Generally, however, unless there is major controversy about what is being said, heads of state are given much more latitude to pass their messages to the public. As noted, the opposition is usually given a chance to respond but being able to respond to an event is very different than being able to initiate it. One has to add to all this the ability to produce endless amounts of soft stories such as the media frenzy that accompanied the debate about which dog would be lucky enough to be adopted by the Obamas. Dominating the headlines is one of the important advantages that come with political power.

Those with power and resources have the added advantages of being able to hire "spin doctors" who are experts at promoting stories to the news media. While many pundits often exaggerate the influence of these advisors, the ability to place potential news stories in an attractive package does make a difference. Advisors are also experts at preparing stories in ways that make it easier to turn them into news stories. Reporters are always pressed for time. Public relations people make journalists' lives much easier because they provide easy access to information and events, deal with technical details such as lighting and camera angles, and even prepare news releases that need little editing before being turned into news.

Having a large staff and a bit of money also allows powerful political actors to hire a talented web team who are responsible for keeping journalists (and supporters) in the loop and preparing interesting videos for general distribution. This means that political power can also be translated into power over the new Internet-based media.

This doesn't mean that every journalist and news medium will provide positive coverage of such announcements. There are certain newspapers, television stations, and especially blogs that are either generally opposed to the president or certain policies. In addition, journalists often frame stories about the powerful with a certain degree of cynicism and reporters are also always on the lookout for scandals. Powerful leaders also fail, and the media are more than happy to talk about these shortcomings in great detail. Even with regard to negative stories, political power can be critical when it comes to damage control. Reporters who come down too hard on powerful leaders may find themselves at the back of the line for getting information. So journalists have no choice but to think very carefully before they go to war against their most important sources. A White House reporter that reveals a presidential scandal is like a magician who burns himself alive on stage. It's a wonderful trick, but you can only do it once.

The other way to get into the news is through the back door. This door is reserved for weaker political actors who only become newsworthy if they do something especially weird or deviant. The powerful can be pretty boring and still get into the news. But if you are not important you better be interesting.

One way weaker groups become interesting enough to get into the news is to take their clothes off. Naked protests have been carried out by groups ranging from People for the Ethical Treatment of Animals ("I'd rather go naked than wear fur") to firefighters demanding higher wages. Naked protesters are not only deviant enough to be considered news, they also provide great visuals. But like all groups that use exceptional actions to attract media attention, those who undress pay a heavy price in terms of legitimacy. Take, for example, the following two news stories about naked bicyclists. The first took place in Seattle in June 2004 and the second in Denver in June 2009 (it was probably not a total coincidence that both took place in June rather than February).

Naked Bicyclists Ride in Protest Over Environmental Abuse

A group of between 50 and 60 naked bicyclists took to the streets of Seattle on Saturday, and a few were seen in Olympia, police said. The event was a protest but it was not immediately clear whether it was linked to a radical environmentalist group known as the Earth Liberation Front. Protesters in Seattle said that they were protesting the use of cars, which increases pollution... The FBI on Friday warned law enforcement agencies across the country that radical environmentalists might be staging protests this weekend to show their support for a jailed arsonist. The FBI bulletin said the Earth Liberation Front reportedly was planning a "day of action and solidarity" that could include acts of eco-terrorism, according to Tor Bjornstad, a police commander in Olympia, one of the cities mentioned as a likely target.[8]

Boulder Police will be Scrutinizing Naked
Bicyclists in Saturday Protest

The Boulder Police Department has a reminder for riders planning to participate Saturday in the World Naked Bike Ride: Indecent-exposure laws will be enforced. Participants not covering their genitals are subject to arrest and, if convicted under this statute, may be required to register as sexual offenders, the department said in a release Wednesday. The department said it also has reached out to organizers of the event to advise them about ways participants may avoid arrest. These include wearing undergarments that cover genitalia or otherwise obscuring those body parts from public view. Participants are strongly urged to be mindful of the requirements of the law.[9]

Both news stories put a special emphasis on what can be called the "Law and Order" frame. In the Seattle story the bicyclists were probably protesting against car pollution and were somehow turned into terrorists (which makes the story far more interesting). The Denver story—which was written before the protest—was initiated by the police and warned protesters that they might be registered as sex offenders. These two stories exemplify two major modes for covering these types of protests: they are covered as either weird, dangerous, or both.

The fact that journalists often focus on the issue of law and order provides important advantages to the authorities because this often fits the message they are promoting. In many conflicts the weaker side (let's call them the challenger) is attempting to talk about some type of injustice while the more powerful side wants to stress the need for law and order. This is true about workers' strikes, protests about issues such as discrimination and human rights, and even when a weaker country (say Iran) challenges a more powerful country (the U.S.). The challenger wants to talk about their demands while the news media are interested in the action. When workers shut down an airline, the major part of the story has to do with the masses of people stranded at airports; the workers' demands for more money are neither interesting nor photogenic. The same is true when protesters use some form of disorder to attract media attention. Any damage they cause is far more newsworthy than the stories they tell about the dangers of (say) global warming. Whatever the personal sympathies of the reporters the old adage remains true: "if it bleeds it leads."

Now to be fair, not every protest gets negative coverage. If, for example, a group can mobilize a very large demonstration for what is generally seen as a legitimate cause, journalists are much more likely to provide sympathetic coverage. In these cases it is the size of the protest that provides the necessary drama. But here, too, only the more powerful political movements can pull off an event of that magnitude and even they can't do it too often. Any publicity they achieve is likely to be fleeting.

Another problem of getting in the news through the back door is that even if you've only put on a weird costume to get in, you're not allowed to change clothes once you get inside. So there you are being filmed in a Polar Bear costume to protest global warming. You want to talk about the environment and the reporters keep asking you about the costume ("How hot is it in there"?). If you decide you've had enough and step outside to change into a jacket and tie, you won't be allowed back in the news room. Peering through the small, dirty window above the locked door in the back you find you've been replaced by naked jugglers protesting prayer in schools.

Is there a Side Door?

There is one strategy that weaker groups can sometime use to provide news people with drama without completely sacrificing legitimacy: *civil disobedience*. Take, for example, a sit-in that blocks an entrance to a factory accused of polluting the water in a particular city. This too is an act of disorder but being dragged off or beaten by police can turn the protesters into victims rather than aggressors. This tactic provides drama with a minimal amount of downside. The relative success of such tactics depends on three factors: the level of violence that the authorities use against the group, the extent to which people can identify with your cause, and the level of violence you use. If you decide to block a road in order to get a raise in salary, for example, you'll probably be covered as a bunch of trouble makers. This is a reminder of how political context and breadth of support can make a major difference in news coverage.

One of the most successful examples of the civil disobedience strategy was used in the civil rights struggle in the 1960s. Martin Luther King had stressed to his followers and the public that the struggle for racial equality would be nonviolent. Even when the protesters were beaten with clubs they refused to respond in kind. An historic protest took place in Birmingham, Alabama, on May 4, 1963. The Police Commissioner Eugene "Bull" Conner decided to set attack dogs on the protesters leading to some terrible pictures of police brutality. One of the most famous pictures was published on the front page of the *New York Times* and showed a fifteen-year old boy being viciously attacked by German Shepherds.[10]

In an important book on the role of the press in the civil rights struggle, Gene Roberts and Hank Klibanoff described the impact the photos had on the political environment surrounding the struggle.

> The police response and the images it produced had an instant impact in two places where it mattered most, Birmingham and Washington. In Birmingham Negro leaders who had been negotiating quietly with moderate whites and who had been reluctant to support [Martin Luther] King quickly fell in line behind him… The images had a far more important impact in Washington… That afternoon, [President John] Kennedy sent Burke Marshall of the Justice Department's civil rights division to Birmingham.[11]

The fact that the civil rights movement received so much sympathetic coverage was much more than a question of mere strategy. It was also a reflection of the fact that American public opinion about race issues was beginning to change.

This was a case where journalists—at least in the North—were making editorial *choices* to cover the story as a clear case of injustice. It tells us that, despite the close association between power and media access, there are cases in which the news media play a more independent role in political conflicts. We also learn that shocking visual images can have an important effect on the political process and that this was true even before the creation of the Internet and YouTube.

Cumulative Inequality

Another ramification of our first principle is the idea of *cumulative inequality.*[12] Not only does political power translate to power over the media, but the political actors who most need access to the news are the ones that find it the most difficult to obtain. As in many areas of life, when it comes to exposure in the news media, the rich generally get richer and the poor remain poor. Those with real political power certainly enjoy getting good publicity (who doesn't?) and it also helps them achieve their political goals. But because they *have* power, they are less *dependent* on the news media than others; they can get things done directly (say by passing a law or sending troops somewhere).

The powerless, on the other hand, have little chance of achieving anything without some public attention. It doesn't matter if it is a protest group trying to recruit members, a member of the political opposition who is trying to speak out against the government, a third party presidential candidate trying to get on the ballot, or a developing country launching a campaign to attract tourism. In each of these cases getting into the news is essential to their cause. But these are the actors who are the least likely to be invited to attend the party; the only way they can get in is if they hide inside the cake and jump out when least expected.

To illustrate this point let's think about two organizations who are pressuring the government concerning different pieces of legislation. One is Microsoft who is concerned about a new law that will limit its ability to include its software as part of every computer that is sold. The other is the Ostrich Liberation League (OLL) who is attempting to get a law passed that makes it illegal to sell ostrich meat, to ride ostriches, or to produce ostrich saddles or hats.

Microsoft has enormous resources that can allow it to work almost entirely behind the scenes using an army of lawyers, lobbyists, and maybe even a few politicians who have received campaign support. From Microsoft's perspective, the less the press writes about the issue the better. The OLL, on the other hand, has no chance at all of getting anywhere unless they attract media attention. But let's face it, Ostriches will never be considered big news. The only way the OLL will get into the news is by doing something outrageous knowing full well that they will be covered as a bunch of wacky eccentrics, to put it mildly.

It is important to emphasize that the level of power should be seen as a continuum rather than a dichotomy. While this discussion has referred to the powerful and the powerless, the truth is that there are political organizations, interest groups, and think tanks that fall somewhere in between these two extremes. The ability of these various actors to promote themselves to the media without resorting to extreme tactics is directly related to their place on the power continuum.

In general however, the news media are major agents for maintaining and even intensifying the power gaps in society. The rules of access insure that the powerful are constantly seen as more important and in many cases more respectable than the weak. This in turn makes it easier for them to maintain or change their preferred policies. As discussed, these rules are not set in stone. There are times when the news media serve as advocates of the weak. This will become much clearer in Chapter 2.

What About the New Media?

Some readers probably think that everything said to this point is simply out of date. They would argue that in the age of cell phones with cameras, YouTube, and the Blogosphere political power becomes less important. Today, even the weakest groups can get their message out to everyone through the Internet and social networking platforms. All it takes is for one good political story to go viral and everyone—including the mainstream media—is paying attention.

The new technology does make a difference, sometimes even a huge difference. But in addition to the new opportunities that have become available because of the new media, there are also some important limitations. The new advantages and the limitations of this new technology can be understood by looking at the type of challenger that could most benefit from these changes: political movements.

Political Movements and the New Media

Most political movements are the classic "back door" challengers. Even the largest movements are usually not considered inherently newsworthy. They still must do something dramatic if they hope to get covered by the traditional media and, as said, this more often than not translates into negative coverage. The question that needs to be asked is how much the new communication technology changes the ability of these movements to become more powerful, to get their message out to supporters and the general public, and to bring about political change.

There are four major goals political movements attempt to achieve where the new Internet media could be useful. The first, and most obvious, is that it should help movements in their efforts to mobilize supporters to their cause. The second goal is to have their messages and news stories appear in the traditional media which will allow them to reach a much wider audience. Related to that amplification effect, the third goal is to have an influence on public opinion so the wider audience becomes more sympathetic with the movement. And ultimately, the fourth is to have an impact on politics. These four goals can be seen as four stations that movements have to pass in their attempts to climb an extremely steep mountain whose peak is called political success. It turns out that not only does it become increasingly difficult to pass each station, but one finds that the new technology becomes less and less helpful as one gets closer to the top.

The first station movements need to pass has to do with their ability to mobilize supporters and other resources in order to become more powerful. Here is where political movements receive their greatest boost from the new media technology. Here, the changes that have taken place with the advent of the new media are nothing short of revolutionary. The Internet and SMS technology provides movements with the potential to communicate instantly with millions of people around the world. Compare the cost and effectiveness of mailing leaflets to supporters as opposed to sending out emails that include both a video presentation and the opportunity to respond to what they've received. Think about the ability to remind people continually of a protest taking place, of being able to ask people to electronically sign a petition and pass it on to their friends, of allowing people to make a donation using a credit card while sitting in their pajamas in front of the computer, or of sending an inspiring speech by your leader to people living in thirty different countries. Now let's supercharge all of this by allowing every movement to put links on its web site that allows it to communicate and build coalitions with other similar movements around the country and the world. When you put all of these assets together you begin to understand the potential the new media represent for mobilizing people and groups for the cause.

The major thing to remember is that all of this revolutionary technology provides movements with the *potential* to exponentially increase their membership and resources. Whether it actually does depends, among many other things, on how much the movement's messages and leaders resonate with a large segment of the public. Here too it's a question of political context. There are tens of thousands of movements demanding our attention. The amount of time and attention any of us can or will devote to any one movement is still extremely limited. Thus, even if a movement has the best technology available it will remain small and obscure unless it appeals to a relatively large number of people who are willing to devote time and money to the cause. Even in the digital age, it is hard to get Americans excited about the preservation of historical sites in Albania.

Movement leaders also find that the fact that people are willing to sign an electronic petition about something does not mean they will either give money or come to a demonstration. In fact, because electronic participation is so easy it may give some people a sense that "they've done their part" and thus even lower the number of people who are willing to get out of their pajamas and do something active for the movement. Perhaps it is no coincidence that in May 2009 one of the oldest American social activists, Ralph Nader, made an extremely aggressive attack on Internet activism. He called the Internet "a huge waste of trivial time." He asked his audience of college students to consider what they were going to tell their grandchildren:

> You know. The world is melting down. They're nine years old. They're sit-
> ting on your lap. They've just become aware of things that are wrong in the

world: starvation, poverty, whatever. And they ask you, what were you doing when all this was happening: Grandma? Grandpa? That you were too busy updating your profile on Facebook ?[13]

A similar point was made by Evgeny Morozov who coined an extremely useful term for this: *slacktivism*.[14] Slacktivism is a combination of the word slacker and activism. The idea is that there are quite a number of digital activities people can carry out that make them feel good about themselves but have absolutely no impact on either society or politics. One of the examples he gives is a Facebook group called "Saving the Children of Africa." Morozov points out that at first glance the organization looks very impressive because it has over 1.2 million members. At the time he wrote however, the organization had raised a paltry $6,000 (about a half a penny a person). As he puts it: "The problem, however, is that the granularity of contemporary digital activism provides too many easy way-outs: too many people decide to donate a penny where they may otherwise want to donate a dollar."[15]

As we move up the mountain of political success, the air gets increasingly thin and the new technology becomes much less helpful. The reason can be summed up in one word: *competition*. Consider attempting to just get past the second station of trying to get favorable coverage of your group in the traditional media. Generating buzz on the Internet about your cause can certainly make a difference, but it is no substitute for generating an investigative report on *CBS Evening News* or *Sixty Minutes*. There are tens of thousands of politicians, organizations, movements, companies, and (let us not forget) celebrities all competing to make it into these news and current events programs. All of these competitors use Twitter and many of them can use the new technology to produce newsworthy events. But the traditional media still have only so much space and time to allocate, even if their web sites provide more space than in the past. Younger journalists probably spend more time actively searching political blogs and Internet sites but they too only have so much time and energy to look. And guess what? They will be especially interested in spending time trying to find stories about the politically powerful.

It also turns out that only a small fraction of major news stories come from the blogosphere. Researchers Jure Leskovec, Lars Backstrom, and Jon Kleinberg employed a powerful computer program to search the web over a fairly large period of time to study the rise and fall of the biggest news stories.[16] They tracked an amazingly large 1.6 million mainstream media sites and blogs. The finding that is most relevant to this discussion was that a mere 3.5 percent of all major news cycles were initiated in the blogosphere and then moved to the other media. The vast majority of news stories ran in the opposite direction: the blogs and alternative news sites were following stories that first appeared in the traditional news media. This should tell you something important about how difficult it is for all political actors to use the new media as a means of breaking into the mainstream media. It should also tell you that traditional media remains the best tool for generating political waves about an issue.

The competition becomes even fiercer when an organization attempts to move beyond gaining news coverage and attempts to interest the broad public or to get policy makers to actually make changes. Starting with having an impact on public opinion, it is almost impossible for a small group to be heard above the crowd. There are, of course, people—you know who you are—who spend hours every day reading political blogs. But even they have no choice but to confine themselves to those issues that interest them. In that case, we are moving from the age of broadcasting to what many have called *narrowcasting*.

Getting the attention of political leaders and policy makers is even harder and needless to say they have their own agendas to promote. Here's a good example that comes from Amnesty International working in Britain. I interviewed one of the people involved in media relations, and he was talking about both the great advantages provided by the web and some limitations. As an example of some of the problems he faced, he talked about an electronic petition they had organized against an anti-terrorism law that allowed the police to lock up terrorist suspects for six weeks before they have to charge them with any offense. They organized a fairly successful campaign to get people to sign a petition on the Prime Minister's web site. The Amnesty spokesperson talked about his frustration.

> We got a reasonable number of people to sign up. The failure was that there were so many populist issues that are being petitioned and we were maybe the 15th most popular. Some of the things that were more popular than us were ridiculous. One of them was whether to allow the Red Arrows [a display troop of the Royal Aircraft] to fly over London to mark the Olympics. The other had to do with demanding that a right-wing television presenter who had a show about cars became Home Secretary [one of the Ministers]. It was a joke and it received I think 5 times as many signatures as we did.[17]

Perhaps a metaphor would be helpful. Your organization has just purchased a megaphone so your leaders will be especially loud. The problem is that every group has a megaphone. To make things worse, those with political power not only have more megaphones, they also have sophisticated sound systems so their speeches are heard all over the country.

Despite all these limitations, there are two very different types of movements who seem to have benefited the most from the emergence of the Internet. The first are what are known as Transnational Advocacy Networks (TANs). Groups dealing with climate change, the dangers of globalization, nuclear proliferation, cruelty to animals, and human rights are all examples of movements who have far more power and influence now than in the past because of their ability to mobilize supporters and resources from around the world. Researchers, governments, and international companies have all begun to think about how these groups' increasing power is having an impact on the world. In fact researchers Sean Aday and Steve Livingston even go so far as to claim that in some cases the impact of these movements can be compared to that of countries.[18]

The second type of group that has seen a major change in their fortunes due to the Internet is terrorist organizations. The Internet provides these groups with a number of important advantages.[19] Terrorist organizations can instantly exchange information—including technical information about weapons—from and to any place on the planet. They can also distribute inspirational material and videos to supporters and potential supporters. The videos can include inspiring speeches from their leaders, threats to carry out terrorist attacks, and actual footage from the attacks they have carried out. Because such videos are considered newsworthy many Western journalists end up showing them to the broader public and in doing so unintentionally help the terrorists spread fear.

The Internet can also be used by terrorists to coordinate tactics and strategy. One of the most important traits of the Internet is that individuals around the world can create *communities* that give them a sense of belonging. While this can, in most cases, be seen as a positive development there are some communities the world could live without. The reason why terrorist groups are especially likely to be empowered by the new media is because mobilization—especially international mobilization—is such a central element in their overall strategy. Unlike more conventional movements, they are not usually attempting to convince the broad public or Western leaders about the legitimacy of their cause. Their goals are to intimidate their opponents. Terrorist groups don't enter the news media through the back door they simply blow it open.

The Internet also provides terrorists with an extremely effective and anonymous method for doing strategic research before an attack. A good example of this new found power can be seen in the report about the planning of the 9/11 attack that was published by the National Commission on Terrorist Attacks Upon the United States.[20] The leaders of Al-Qaeda were able to use the Internet to find flight schools that might accept them and to find routes and flight paths of various airlines and of course to communicate with each other. In fact, learning how to use the Internet was an important part of their terrorist training.

So in some ways the new media have radically changed the relationship between political and media power. But due to the rules of political competition, these cases remain the exception rather than the rule. When it comes to the ability of movements and other challengers to organize and mobilize it is certainly a new age. On the other hand, the new technologies appears to be less revolutionary when it comes to getting a message to the broad public or bringing about real change. Equally important, the ability of political actors to successfully exploit the new media depends first and foremost on who they represent, their goals, and the political environment in which they are operating. The powerful, it turns out, still have the upper hand.

So if things are so great for the political powerful, why are they constantly whining about news coverage? It turns out that despite their many advantages even the most powerful lose control over news stories. This brings us to the next part of our story.

Questions for Thought and Discussion

1. Bearing in mind what was said about political power over the news media, record and watch the national or local news on television. How many stories involve powerful people or groups and how many items include weaker actors? What are the differences between the kinds of news stories that are constructed about powerful and less powerful political actors?

2. Think of a political group with which you identify. Based on what you learned in this chapter, think about the following questions: What are some of the activities the group could carry out in order to generate some positive publicity? What are the characteristics of the group that either increase or decrease its chances of getting this type of publicity? Is there anything the group has done that you consider a mistake because of the bad publicity it produced?

2 Political Control and Media Independence

It might seem at this point that those in power have it pretty easy. All they have to do is to send out some press releases and organize some photo opportunities and they have it made. Now while some presidents do enjoy a certain honeymoon during their first few months in office, the halo usually comes off pretty quickly. Think about the final days of the George W. Bush presidency. The news and entertainment media were ruthless in their attacks on Bush, especially when it came to the Iraq war and the horrible state of the economy. It was hard to find many people who would defend him. In fact, one of Senator John McCain's biggest problems in the 2008 elections was to convince people that as a Republican he was "not Bush."

The point to remember is that although political power always provides advantages, the news media sometimes go from being lap dogs to attack dogs. The second principle explains when this happens: *When the authorities lose control over the political environment, they also lose control over the news.*

To clarify, it is helpful to begin with an imaginary situation. The president has decided to declare war on Iran. Due to security concerns he has asked all the reporters who want to cover the story to stay in a secluded site, and their cell phones are confiscated as they enter the hall. The hall was rented by the president's staff, and when he announces that the war has begun he has also filled the room with cheering supporters. Every hour or so one of the president's spokespeople comes in to give the reporters a briefing, which includes some shocking aerial photographs that prove that Iran is building nuclear weapons (the truth is that it is hard to see anything in these types of pictures but the professional analysts are generous enough to tell the reporters what they're looking at). At the same time reporters are getting urgent messages from their editors demanding they send something before deadline. Journalists resent being manipulated in these types of situations, but given the circumstances they have little choice but to prepare a story based on what they've been told.

As the day moves on, however, things begin to change. It turns out that some of the reporters were able to smuggle their Blackberries into the hall. There are some disturbing reports being circulated on the web of an orphanage in Teheran being bombed and dozens of children being killed. The tragic videos from the wreckage were quickly uploaded onto YouTube. In addition reporters are getting text messages from some members of Congress claiming that the president only went to war because of a drop in his approval ratings. By the end of the day, the coverage of the war has become much less enthusiastic and one sided. It is clear that the administration has lost a good deal of control over the story.

As you have no doubt figured out, the hall is a metaphor for the political environment. The political environment is simply a general term for everything that people and groups in a particular place and time are saying and doing about an issue. As an example, think about the ongoing debate in the United States over abortion. If someone wanted to know something about the political environment surrounding abortion at a particular point in time one would first ask whether any political elites were dealing with it. It is especially important to look at those who have relatively easy access to the press: the president, members of the cabinet, members of Congress, senators, governors, political candidates, and various non-governmental elites such as those at top think tanks. We'd also want to know whether there were any major events taking place either in courtrooms, the legislature, or on the part of Pro-Life and Pro-Choice movements. Another thing to look at would be the breakdown of opinions on this sensitive topic among politicians and in the general public. Journalists construct news stories about an issue by turning to their usual elite sources and trying to gauge the public mood about the topic. In a sense every piece of "data" they collect provides them with clues about the state of the political environment.

When asking about level of control over the political environment, what is meant by the term *the authorities*? In some situations this could be the president. In others it could be the mayor, government, the prime minister or even the king (it's good to be king). All of these political leaders spend most of their time attempting to take control of a situation by doing things like speaking publicly about an issue, by promoting new legislation or regulations, by persuading and pressuring various elites to support their policies, and by communicating with the press. This is what it means to be a political leader; you lead by constantly attempting to move policies that are important to you in a particular direction. The principle that is being dealt with in this chapter tells us that the more leaders succeed in all of these efforts concerning a particular issue the better they will be at determining how the press will cover their positions and their actions.

The best way to understand the notion of a leaders' political control is to look at three major indicators of success. The first is the extent to which they are able to take control over *important events*. Going back to the fictitious war on Iran, the fact that an orphanage was bombed is a good example of what happens when the authorities lose control over events. Wars never go exactly as planned and the more mistakes and accidents that take place the more difficult it becomes to portray the war effort as a success. When civilians are killed it puts presidents and prime ministers on the defensive and they are forced to spend a good deal of their time dealing with "damage control." These types of situations severely limit their ability to get their messages through to the news media and to the public. The same can be said about more routine political events such as a president's legislation being defeated in Congress.

The second factor is the ability of the authorities to take control over the *flow of information*. This is why the president, who was declaring war on Iran, was so anxious to get the journalists in a closed room with no access to the outside world. When you have a monopoly on the major commodity journalists are anxious to buy (information), you can pretty much set your own price. In the digital age it has become increasingly difficult for even the most ruthless dictators to completely control the flow of information. Nevertheless, there are some types of events—such as secret negotiations—where the president and other leaders find it easier to control the flow of information. This is why *leaks* are so good for journalists and so bad for leaders. Leaks are especially problematic for the authorities because they are often designed to embarrass those in charge.

An important illustration of the difficulties modern leaders face in the digital age comes from the release of the hundred of thousands of documents first released by WikiLeaks in the course of 2010. Among the most embarrassing revelations was the fact that Pakistan, which was receiving more than a billion dollars a year in U.S. aid was secretly aiding Afghani insurgents in their efforts to defeat NATO troops.[1] Stories released in December of that year also revealed that Yemen had taken responsibility for U.S. missile attacks on suspected terrorists in Yemen and that Saudi Arabia was pressuring the U.S. to bomb Iran.[2] A significant controversy emerged about whether such leaks were ethically acceptable or legal. One fact however has become indisputable: Modern leaders have to assume that anything that is put in writing can eventually be made public.

The third factor that tells us something important about the control over the political environment may be the most important: how much are leaders able to *mobilize a broad consensus in support of their policies*, especially among the political elite. The reason why it is especially important to look at the level of consensus among the elite is that these are the major sources for journalists. Journalists spend most of their time either with elites or with each other. The only way journalists can know what the public thinks is to look at polls.

There are some events that automatically lead to a wide consensus, and presidents always look better when everyone agrees with them. Leaders usually receive the highest level of political support during times of crisis. Think about the political environment surrounding George W. Bush after the 9/11 attacks on the Twin Towers. It would have been hard to find an American who did not want to strike back against the terrorists; Bush had few difficulties finding support for his war against Al-Qaeda and their protectors, the Taliban in Afghanistan. The U.S. news media, needless to say, were also in full support, not only in editorials but also in the way they covered the issue.

There are a number of reasons why the press is so sensitive to the level of consensus about an issue. The first is that when those in the opposition are unwilling to come out publically against the president, the journalists have no critics to quote. Reporters depend on their sources to tell them whether an issue is considered controversial. In addition if "everyone important" agrees on a certain policy, the chances are that most reporters feel the same way. This is especially true when the country comes together after an attack such as 9/11.

There is nothing more unifying than having a common enemy, especially if that enemy has just murdered thousands of your own countrymen. Finally, when the vast majority of the public supports the president it makes absolutely no economic sense for journalists to run in the opposite direction. This last point reminds us that journalists, despite their over reliance on elite sources also have to take public opinion into account. News is, in the end, a business and the last thing you want to do is annoy your clients.

Political Control and Media Independence

What do we mean when we talk about the "an independent media"? To answer that question you should think about three points on a continuum. At one end of this line (let's put it on the right), one would find those situations in which the news media are completely dependent on the authorities for everything they report. This is most likely to take place when presidents declare war on another country. Presidents in these situations have a large amount of political support and unless they lose control over events, journalists are hanging on their every pronouncement and move. During a crisis the news media are often at their most dependent.

At the other end of this continuum (say the extreme left point on the line) are the situation in which the news media exhibit the highest level of independence, when they become true watchdogs. These are those rare cases where instead of being dependent on elite sources they *initiate* or uncover critical news stories on their own. The clearest cases have to do with investigative journalism in which journalists uncover a scandal of some kind that embarrasses the authorities or even weakens them politically. While such news stories are pretty common when it comes to local politicians, finding dirt on the president or on those in the highest echelons of government without the aid of other elites is much rarer.

The middle point on the continuum refers to those situations in which the news media are getting a substantial amount of information that contradicts the official line concerning an issue. This happens when authorities only have partial control over the political environment. In the hypothetical example about a war with Iran this occurred when journalists started finding out about opinions (from the opposition) and events (the bombing of an orphanage) that contradict what the administration is telling them. In these situations the news media exhibit partial independence because although they no longer depend exclusively on the authorities, they still depend on the opposition to provide an alternative view. In these situations the issue has become controversial and the political debate itself becomes an important part of new stories.

The best known example of investigative reporting is the Watergate scandal. This was a story that was continually pushed by *Washington Post* reporters Bob Woodward and Carl Bernstein and many other reporters that eventually led to President Richard Nixon's resignation from office. It is true that the reporters may not have gotten very far without the help of the source known as "Deep Throat" (who many years later was revealed to be Deputy Director of the FBI

Mark Felt Sr.). It is tempting to say that even this example begins with a political initiative because Felt held a grudge against the president (not being promoted). But let's give this one to the press.

There are two other historical scandals that the media uncovered that are worth mentioning: The Iran-Contra affair that embarrassed President Ronald Reagan and the Monica Lewinsky scandal that seriously damaged the Clinton presidency. The Iran-Contra affair began when the Lebanese magazine *Ash-Shiraa* reported in November of 1986 that the Reagan administration had agreed to sell arms to Iran in an effort to release American hostages. The Contra part of the scandal comes from the fact that the money gained from the sales went to a right-wing guerilla group (the "Contras") trying to overturn the Nicaraguan government. While President Regan survived the scandal, it left a permanent stain on his administration. This was one of those rare occasions when the press uncovered a story without depending on the opposition to initiate it.

In terms of press independence, the case of Monica Lewinsky is somewhat more muddled. The scandal had to do with Clinton's affair with a twenty-two-year old intern. In addition to the fact that he was cheating on his wife, his attempts to deny the relationship only made things worse ("I did not have sexual relations with that woman"). As an aside, it's sort of ironic that Iran Contra is called an *affair,* but what happened with Monica Lewinsky was referred to as a *scandal.* The scandal was initially exposed by the web based Drudge Report in 1998, which reported that *Newsweek* was sitting on the story.[3] It was certainly a major achievement for the online media. Matt Drudge prides himself on reporting on issues and events that are ignored by the mainstream press. On the other hand, one of the main reasons why the scandal became so serious was that it was picked up by Clinton's political opponents who were able to exploit the story for some time. Clinton was eventually impeached for perjury and obstruction of justice but then acquitted by the Senate. The news media were the ones to initiate the story, but it took a massive political effort for the process to get as far as it did.

The news media can also exhibit independence from the authorities in ways that are not related to scandals. A good example was an exposé conducted by the *Washington Post* in published in the summer of 2010 that looked at the massive expansion of the U.S. intelligence community after 9/11.[4] It was just the type of critical analysis one would want from a news medium that saw itself as a government watchdog. The problem is that as news divisions find it increasingly difficult to turn a profit such investigative reporting is becoming increasingly rare. Investigative journalism costs a great deal of money because while the reporters are working on the story they are not contributing to the daily production of news.

There are, of course, endless stories that embarrass the presidency or the cabinet based on stupid, foolish, or controversial things said or done. This is especially true during election campaigns (Obama during the 2008 campaign: "I've now been in 57 states—I think I have one left to go").[5] These incidents are passing moments in the world of infotainment and rarely last for more than a few days. The true power of an independent news media can only be demonstrated through news stories that have a significant impact on the political process.

Evidence about the rarity of truly independent and powerful news stories can be found by carrying out a search on Google of major events of the last decade. Look for any historical timeline that lists the major events of the last decade. You will find elections and election campaigns (2000, 2004), wars (Iraq and Afghanistan), terrorist attacks (9/11, attacks in Europe), natural disasters (the Asian tsunami, hurricane Katrina, the earthquake in Haiti), major accidents (the BP oil spill) international conflicts (the United States and Iran, the Middle East conflict), Olympics and other major sporting events (Super Bowl, the World Cup), and economic crashes (the Great Recession of 2008). What you will probably not find is a single major event *initiated* by the news media.

Once again, this does not mean that the news media do not play an important role in politics (otherwise why write a book about it). What it means is that the news media spend the vast majority of time transforming events that are initiated by others. This is why it is so important to look first at what is happening in the political world in order to understand how the news media cover issues and events.

Media and War

One of the most important areas where one can see the clear relationship between political control and control over the news has to do with the role the media play in wars. The coverage of wars is a topic that often ignites passions both because the stakes are so high because when things go wrong many blame the press. When things go well, on the other hand, the political and military leaders are more than happy to take the credit. When the press treat these leaders as heroes, well that's obviously the one time the media got it right.

When trying to understand the role the news media play in war it is always helpful to begin by looking at *different* wars and *different stages* of war. The reason is that sometimes the authorities have a great deal of control over the political environment and sometimes they don't. If you pay attention to this, you will understand why the news media sometimes provide a great deal of support for the president's policies and at other times they make the leader's life downright miserable.

I'm going to talk about three wars: Vietnam (1965–975), the Gulf War with Iraq (1991), and the Iraq War that began in 2003. The fact that each of these wars involved a different president is important because any problems they had with the media cannot be attributed to mere bias (unless you believe the news media hate *all* presidents).

The reason for starting with the Vietnam War is that this was the first time when the role of the media became so controversial. It was the first war that received independent TV coverage, and one of the myths that emerged at the time was that U.S. had lost the war *because* of the media. In fact there are some people in the Pentagon who probably still believe that to be the case.

The claim was that because this was the first time Americans were seeing the horrors of war, public support for the war was constantly eroding. Those who have done serious research on the topic, however, have come to a very different conclusion.[6] It was the political environment surrounding the war that changed first; the change in news coverage reflected what was happening among the elite in America.

In the early stages of the Vietnam War there was a tremendously high level of consensus surrounding the conflict and the American news media was more than happy to provide suitable levels of enthusiasm. The reason for this broad support was that at the time the Cold War with the Soviet Union was high on the U.S. political agenda; the Vietnam War was seen as an essential battle to stop the spread of communism. An important book on this topic by Daniel Hallin showed that the vast majority of news from those early years fully supported the war effort.[7] Even the liberal *New York Times* published maps with large black arrows of communism descending on South East Asia and large white arrows of the free world coming up to stop them. Those few people who opposed the war were covered as either "hippies," "yippies," or "communist sympathizers."

Hallin found that U.S. coverage did become more critical of the government and the military as the war dragged on. So what changed? The first thing that changed was that it became increasingly clear to quite a few people that America was simply not winning the war. All this time, the U.S. military was continually making optimistic predictions about the end "being in sight." But the number of American dead and wounded continued to rise and the horrible cost of the war became increasingly apparent. Journalists seeing what was happening on the battlefield became increasing skeptical that this was true. Neither the political nor the military authorities were able to take control over the events surrounding the war.

The military also had little control over the *flow of information* about the conflict, even though this was long before the creation of the Internet. It may be hard to believe, but there was no censorship during the Vietnam War; reporters could pretty much go wherever they wanted and report as they saw fit. This was not a problem in the beginning when journalists were supportive, but it became a continual irritant for the military as the tone turned more negative.

Eventually the political climate surrounding the war began to change and people considered "serious" by the news media were raising questions about whether the war was winnable. This included not only academics (who were usually considered hippies with ties), but also senators, business people, and even people in the military (who almost always spoke off the record). Journalists were also changing their own opinions, in part because of what they were seeing and hearing in the field. The point is that President Johnson was losing control over the level of consensus surrounding the war. As Hallin formulated it the Vietnam news story moved from the "sphere of consensus" to the "sphere of legitimate controversy." Once an issue is considered controversial, current events programs feel an obligation to bring both sides of the argument (although almost never *more* than two sides because that confuses people).

The best known tale about the changing political climate has to do with a special CBS broadcast on the Vietnam War by Walter Cronkite that took place on February 27, 1968. For younger readers it is worth mentioning that Cronkite was considered the most important news anchor on television and enjoyed an impeccable reputation for professionalism and objectivity. Cronkite was reporting on the Tet Offensive, which was considered by many a military failure for the United States. Many viewers were shocked when Cronkite—who was as far from a hippie as one could get—concluded his report by suggesting that the Vietnam War could not be won and that the United States would have to find a way out. As David Halberstam put it: "it was the first time in American history a war had been declared over by an anchorman."[8] The best part of this now classic story is that President Lyndon Johnson reportedly reacted to the broadcast by saying: "If I've lost Cronkite, I've lost Middle America."[9]

The Politics-Media-Politics Cycle

A good way to understand what happens when leaders lose control over the political environment is to think of it as a cycle: political change leads to changes in the way the news media cover issues which leads to further political change. This is the Politics-Media-Politics (PMP) cycle. This idea will be helpful for explaining quite a few things throughout the book.

Here's how this works when it comes to changes in political consensus. There is, for example, a change in the amount of consensus surrounding a policy (less support for the Vietnam War among the elite). This leads to a change in the way the media cover it (more negative coverage such as the Cronkite report), which leads to further changes in the political environment (more people opposing the war). If we understand these types of changes as a cycle, we begin to realize that *the news media do not merely reflect political change, in many cases they can magnify and accelerate change.* As the coverage of the Vietnam War grew more negative, an increasing number of Americans were being asked to "take sides," whereas before there was only one side to take. When this type of cycle takes place, more people are willing to come to protests and sign petitions, more people will contribute money to the cause, and a growing number of political leaders will feel comfortable publicly opposing the war.

The same PMP process can also be used to explain the changing media coverage of the Iraq War in 2003. When the Bush administration declared war on Iraq there was a fairly large consensus in favor and there were few leaders in either party who opposed the need to use force to remove Saddam Hussein's weapons of mass destruction (which in the end were not there). Even if some journalists had doubts about the reasons for going to war, there were very few credible sources they could turn to find opposing views. Here too there was little political debate about the issue and the news media reflected and probably even reinforced that consensus. There is a revealing quote about how this works from Ted Koppel from *Nightline* that appeared in a book by Kristina Borjesson about the performance of American journalists at that time:

I as a reporter have to say, "Here is what the President is saying. Here is what the Secretary of Defense is saying. Here is what the director of the CIA is saying. Here is what the members of Congress are saying. And indeed, when everyone at that point who has access to the classified information is with more or less one voice agreeing that, yes there appears to be evidence that Saddam Hussein still has weapons of mass destruction—maybe not nuclear, but certainly chemical and probably biological—are you suggesting that the entire American press corps then say: "Well, horse manure?"[10]

But if the press is truly supposed to be a government watchdog shouldn't journalists be the ones to lead the pack, rather than follow it? Even if some would like that to happen, only exceptionally brave reporters will risk being called traitors in times of war. Consider the comments by former White House correspondent Elizabeth Bumiller, speaking a year after the Iraq war began about the press conference where Bush told the country about going to war:

I think we were very deferential because in the East Room press conference, it's live. It's very intense. It's frightening to stand up there. I mean think about it. You are standing up on prime time live television, asking the President of the United States a question when the country is about to go to war. There was a serious, somber tone that evening, and I think it made—and you know, nobody wanted to get into an argument with the president at this very serious time. It had a very heavy feeling of history to it, that press conference.[11]

The PMP cycle is an ongoing process (think PMPMPMP…) in which at each stage political actors and journalists feed off of one another. In the early stages of the Iraq War, the U.S. military had a good deal of control as they fought their way into Baghdad. They also had little problem with taking control over the flow of information because many of the reporters were "embedded" with the troops. The idea of embedding is that journalists are attached to military units. On the one hand, this gives them some great visuals and live reports from combat zones. However, there are serious problems with embedding that provides advantages to the military. It is much easier for the military to control reporters because the military decides exactly what they are allowed to see. In addition, by having journalists focus on specific battles they are less likely to deal with bigger issues. Finally, journalists who spend a good deal of time with the soldiers tend to identify with them (especially if they come under fire together). Some of you may have noticed that the word embedded sounds a lot like "in bed with" and maybe there's a good reason for that.

Once the "army versus army" part of the Iraq war was over, the American military began to lose control over events. The insurgents (as they came to be called) were able to kill thousands of soldiers and civilians, and it soon became clear that the war was going to continue for some time. This led to more political leaders speaking out against the war. The deteriorating situation also led to journalists increasingly reporting on the dissent and to begin—as in Vietnam—to be more skeptical about the optimistic reports they were getting from the government. This change in coverage no doubt helped accelerate the level and intensity of opposition (the PMP cycle at work). Many people depend on the news media as a barometer of political change, and as the story goes negative, people need less courage to express anti-war sentiments.

Although such changes in public sentiment usually take place over an extended period of time, they can lead to some very dramatic changes in the political environment. One way to understand which direction the political wind is blowing is to ask, "who is on the defensive?" By the end of 2006, Bush found himself continually on the defensive about the war, especially when his critics reminded people of his landing on an American aircraft carrier accompanied by a huge banner: "Mission Accomplished."[12] Another sign of the change in the political climate was that in the 2008 primaries Barack Obama's early opposition to the war became an asset while Hillary Clinton was forced to defend herself to the Democratic base for supporting the invasion of Iraq.[13]

Now, to better understand the importance of how control over the political environment has an impact on the media we need to go back in time to 1991. That was the time of the Gulf War when the *first* President Bush went to war against Iraq. As a reminder, the spark that led to war was when Iraq invaded and occupied neighboring Kuwait and annexed it to Iraq. President Bush and most of the world reacted angrily to this open act of aggression. The president formed a large coalition of thirty-four countries in order to kick Iraq out of Kuwait.[14]

The reason it's worth making the trip back in time to deal with this conflict is that in this case the change in the political environment ran in exactly the *opposite* direction than in either Vietnam or later the Iraq war. The issue of whether to pursue the first war against Iraq was at *first controversial* and then became *consensual*. The PMP cycle stills works but here as time moves on the authorities gain *more* control over the political environment which leads to *more supportive media coverage* which leads to *more political support*. It is important to have this type of example in order to show that time does not *always* work against political leaders.

At first President H.W. Bush faced quite a bit of opposition for his decision to use military force to free Kuwait. In fact the vote to approve using military force against Iraq only passed the Senate by a margin of 52–47.[15] The fact that the issue was controversial led to plenty of dissenting voices being heard in the news media. A study carried out by ADT research made a distinction between two types of television news stories that appeared before the outbreak of the war.[16] "Controversy" stories were those that focused on the debate about whether to use military force against Iraq while "Yellow Ribbon" stories were those that centered more on how the troops were getting ready for war (which provided the U.S. military with considerable space for telling their story). In the time leading up to the war the Controversy stories outnumbered Yellow Ribbon stories by 45 to 8.

Once the war began however, the political climate surrounding the war became extremely supportive and it was difficult to find any criticisms in either the Congress or the news media. Now it was a question of who supported the troops and nobody wanted to be on the wrong side of that issue. This reluctance to oppose the president became even stronger when it became clear that the war was going to be a great success with a minimal number of American casualties. A journalist based in Washington was asked whether or not it was easier to find oppositional voices before the war broke out:

> Yes, because more people had opinions. There were more critics, critics in the Congress, critics in the think tanks. But once there was a declaration of war basically because Congress voted and the U.S. committed its young men and women to fight, the critics were no longer critical. They immediately turned to support the Commander and Chief. In some ways it was a nice thing to see and feel but if the war would have lasted longer, I think people would have raised more questions about what we were doing.[17]

The last point tells us something important about the role of the media in wars fought by democratic countries. Governments have a much easier time maintaining control over the political environment and the media in a short war. The very fact that a war goes on for a long time—as did the second war with Iraq—is a sign of failure. In addition, the chances that mistakes will be made and that embarrassing information will come out also increases with time. Finally, as the length of a war grows, government critics will inevitably feel less conflicted about coming out against the war.

The role of the news media in the first Iraq war was also illustrative for another reason: the almost complete control the authorities had over events and the flow of information.[18] The Gulf War was simply a success story from beginning to end. The United States was able to push the Iraqi forces out of Kuwait in a very short time and the number of American casualties remained relatively small. It was the high point of the first Bush's presidency. He was not reelected, however, in part because he was unable to maintain control over the area that became the primary issue in the 1992 election: the economy.[19]

When the government has a monopoly on information about events it can make sure that only supportive images and information are released to the media. The Allied forces in the Gulf War had almost everything they could dream of in terms of control over information and events.[20] First, the vast majority of that conflict was an *air* war; the ground offensive only lasted forty-eight hours. The journalists had very little knowledge of what was going on during the bombing raids. They had almost no access to the actual war and were completely dependent on official sources. The military was also very fortunate in that almost all of the reporters were stuck covering the war from Saudi Arabia. There was this vast desert to cross and those that tried either got lost or (in one case) taken prisoner.

This was also near the beginning of what become known as "24 hour news" cycle and CNN became a household word during this war. So the military had an almost limitless *demand* for information and they were the only ones with the ability to *supply* it. This is every informational officer's dream. It is small wonder that the television news of that war had so many inspiring video clips of "smart" bombs despite the fact that most of the bombs were actually pretty dumb.

Let's not forget the other important difference between the two wars with Iraq: one was considered a huge success and the other a potential failure. It is revealing that in the first Gulf War President H.W. Bush *refused* to invade Iraq because he felt the United States might "lose control" over the situation.[21] This is, of course, exactly what happened years later when his son did invade and the number of American losses rose to a level that nobody could have imagined when the war began.

The point to remember is this: when officials lose control over the information and events they also lose control over the news. Lance Bennett makes a similar point in his own work on this topic.[22] He distinguishes between fully controlled news such as press releases, partially controlled news as exemplified by a press conference where reporters ask questions, and uncontrolled news such as when scandals break out. When leaders are able to maintain control of events, take control over the flow formation, and mobilize a high degree elite consensus in support of their policies they have little difficulty taking control over the news.

Technology, News, and Informational Control

The discussion about the importance of taking control over the flow of information brings us back to the question of how the massive technological changes that have taken place in recent years influence the construction of news. Conventional wisdom has it that the increased ability of journalists to gather information and images has made it more difficult for governments to maintain a monopoly over information. When it comes to covering wars, for example, the spread of videophones and extremely easy satellite links means that journalists can send live feeds from all over the battlefield. Steven Livingston and Douglas Van Belle point to the fact that whereas journalists in the first Gulf War in 1991 needed a flat-bed truck and four additional workers to set up a satellite link, a reporter covering the 2003 Iraq could put everything he needed into a carry-on bag small enough to fit into the overhead luggage bin locker of a commercial airline.[23]

These technological changes in how news is collected and distributed have influences that go far beyond the ways in which wars are covered. The fact that every citizen with a cell phone can photograph events as they take place and immediately upload them where millions then can see them tells us we are in a different age. There is also the blogosphere where everyone has the potential to be a journalist, or at the very least a columnist. Let us also not forget that traditional journalists have access through the Internet to a wealth of information that the previous generation of reporters could have only dreamed about.

One way to discuss these changes is to talk about *event-driven journalism*. Regina Lawrence was one of the first to write about this phenomenon.[24] The basic idea is that technological innovations have increased the number of "spontaneous" news stories that are neither planned nor driven by the authorities.

This has to do, among other things with the fact that almost everyone has a camera on their phone and even (or especially) young children know how to upload what's happening onto the Internet. In a sense, everyone has at least the potential to find and record major news stories. In these types of situations some claim that the press has much greater power than in the past to decide which of the many events they are hearing about deserve attention and how they should be covered. In theory, at least, this means that the authorities are increasingly losing control over the political environment and the news media have more opportunities to become independent advocates of a particular story line.

One particularly revealing example of this idea is the Abu Ghraib prison scandal that broke out in April of 2004.[25] Shocking pictures came out at that time showing prisoners in that Iraqi prison who were being tortured by American soldiers. The photos included guards beating prisoners who were handcuffed, a hooded inmate with electrodes hooked up to his fingers, smiling guards posing in front of a "naked pyramid" of prisoners, and soldiers being pulled by the neck with a dog leash. When the story broke these pictures were soon available on the Internet for everyone to see. The Bush administration was put on the defensive, and a public debate ensued as to what types of methods were permissible in interrogating prisoners. The debate over how much force to use in interrogations continued for many years after the incident.

This scandal shows both how technology provides new opportunities for a more independent press and public, but does not completely strip the authorities of their power over the news.[26] On the one hand, the very fact that these disturbing pictures "went viral" meant that the number of Americans and people around the world who were exposed to them was immeasurably higher than would have been the case before the digital age. It is also possible that these pictures would have never seen the light of day in the past. The fact that so many young people, including soldiers, have got into the habit of sending each other pictures through the Internet certainly makes it much more difficult for the authorities to take control over the flow of information.

On the other hand, it is important to keep in mind other details before deciding to give all the credit to the new technology. First, the story was only taken seriously when it was reported by Seymour Hersh in the *New Yorker Magazine* and in a report on *60 Minutes II* that was broadcast on April 28, 2004.[27] This reminds us that unless the traditional news media pick up a story going around the Internet it is unlikely to develop much traction. In any case, as discussed in the last chapter, stories that move *from* the web to the traditional news media are very much the exception rather than the rule.

In addition, once an embarrassing news story like Abu Ghraib becomes an issue, there is always a contest between the government and its opponents about how to think about it. Here we find that even if authorities have lost a certain amount of control over how stories break, they still have a good deal of influence on how they are "framed." The concept of frames will be given a good deal of attention in the next chapter, but for now you can think about political actors attempting to promote a particular storyline to the media and the public.

In a study by Lance Bennett, Regina Lawrence, and Steven Livingston, the researchers were interested in looking at the extent to which the U.S. press tended to frame what was happening "as an isolated case of abuse perpetrated by low-level soldiers" or a policy of "torture."[28] The "Isolated Abuse" frame was the story line promoted by the administration and the "Torture" frame was promoted by many of its critics. The researchers analyzed the content of news stories appearing in the *Washington Post* over an extended time period. They found that 81 percent of the news stories emphasized the "Abuse" frame and only 3 percent talked about torture.

So what's going on here? Even in the new informational era, political power counts for something. In fact, it counts for quite a bit. Even when the powerful are not responsible for initiating a story, it doesn't mean they don't get involved. One of the major advantages for authorities is the fact that the news media routinely turn to them for authoritative information even when they aren't initiating the events. Whether it is a national disaster, a scandal or a foreign conflict, one of the first things journalists will do is to turn to officials and try to get a handle on what's going on, what it means, and what action will be taken.

Good evidence on this point is provided in a study by Steven Livingston and Lance Bennett that looked at how the American news media covered a long list of international news stories that appeared on CNN from 1994 to 2001.[29] The researchers made a critical distinction between institutionally driven news (mostly news initiated by the government), event-driven news without any involvement of officials, and event-driven news with official involvement. As expected there was a serious rise in the number of event-driven news stories. This tells us that the new technology is indeed succeeding in allowing the press greater access to news stories that might have been lost in previous times. Nevertheless, most of these stories included some type of involvement by officials. In their conclusion, Livingston and Bennett put it this way:

> We began this article by asking if event-driven news stories were becoming more numerous and whether they are changing the reliance of journalists on officials in selecting and cueing their political content. The answers seem to be yes and no: *Yes*, event-driven news stories are more common; *no*, officials seem to be as much a part of the news as ever. When an unpredicted, nonscripted, spontaneous event is covered in the news, the one predictable component of coverage is the presence of official sources.[30]

One way to think about this situation is that even when an unexpected story breaks—which is now happening more often—those in power can often *commandeer* the story and move it in their preferred direction. This does not mean they will succeed. There are plenty of political actors who will try to promote their own interpretation to the media. The relative success of the various antagonists will depend in the end on their level of political power and the extent to which they are able to take control over relevant information and events. This reminds us once again that only by looking at the bigger political picture can one really understand the impact these technological changes are likely to have on the media and on the political process.

The New Media and Authoritarian Societies

This book is almost exclusively concerned with the ongoing interactions between media and politics in democracies. The reason is that when the news media have little or no discretion in how they cover an event (which is what happens in non-democratic societies) they become mere amplifiers spreading the leader's messages. Despite this focus on democracies, it is worthwhile taking a small detour to ask whether the development of the Internet has seriously damaged the ability of leaders in non-democratic societies to control the flow of information within their own country and internationally.

One of the best known examples has to do with the Iranian "Twitter" Revolution that took place in June of 2009. President Ahmadinejad had claimed victory in an election that many Iranians and outside observers considered fraudulent. Massive protests erupted in Iran and they met with considerable force by the Iranian security forces. The reason why the revolution became so identified with Twitter was that this was the one social media that the authorities found almost impossible to control. Actually, there were plenty of other media that appeared to be important in keeping the "revolution" alive. Commentators were extremely excited about what was happening in Iran and many suggested (yet again) that a new technologically-driven dawn was breaking. Here is one example taken from a *Washington Times* piece:

> The spirit of liberty finally arrived at Tehran's Freedom Square. Hundreds of thousands of Iranians demonstrated Monday against Friday's election, which handed President Mahmoud Ahmadinejad an improbably lopsided victory… Iran is a highly computer-literate society with a large number of bloggers and hackers. The hackers in particular were active in helping keep channels open as the regime blocked them, and they spread the word about functioning proxy portals. Hackers also reportedly took down Mr. Ahmadinejad's Web site in an act of cyberdisobedience… The immediacy of the reports was gripping. Well-developed Twitter lists showed a constant stream of situation updates and links to photos and videos, all of which painted a portrait of the developing turmoil. Digital photos and videos proliferated and were picked up and reported in countless external sources safe from the regime's Net crackdown. Eventually the regime started taking down these sources, and the e-dissidents shifted to e-mail. The only way to completely block the flow of Internet information would have been to take the entire country offline, a move the regime apparently has resisted thus far.[31]

It seems though that calling what happened a "Twitter Revolution" was a gross exaggeration of what actually happened. While using that label made the story much more dramatic (and great for the Twitter brand) those who looked deeper into the topic were less convinced:

> Iran experts and social networking activists say that while Iranian election protesters have certainly used social media tools, no particular technology has been instrumental to organizers' ability to get people on the street. Indeed, most of the organizing has occurred through far more mundane means: SMS text messages and word of mouth. Sysomos, a Toronto-based Web analytics company that researches social media, says there are only about 8,600 Twitter users whose profiles indicate they are from Iran. "I think the idea of a Twitter revolution is very suspect," says Gaurav Mishra, co-founder of 20:20 WebTech, a company that analyzes the effects of social media. "The amount of people who use these tools in Iran is very small and could not support protests that size."[32]

In theory the new media should be much more important as a form of political communication in societies where the traditional media are controlled by the government. In many cases this is probably true. It would be a mistake however to become overly euphoric about the power of these new communication tools. First, the new media can often be controlled and censored. A good example is what has been called the "Great Firewall of China" that allows the Chinese government to both block and investigate what Internet users are saying and doing. The Iranian example also shows us that political control is the most important determinant of how political uprisings turn out. The Iranian authorities chose to use brute force to quell the revolution by opening fire on the protests. The real problem with Twitter and the other new media is that you can't really use them to shoot back. In addition, while the Internet did allow many Iranian protesters to bring their distress to the outside world, the world had no intention of getting involved. Here too political considerations in the West were far more important than the shocking images coming out of Iran.

Interestingly, one of the most important technological changes in this area is not based on the Internet: satellite television. The most well known example of a satellite news station is Al Jazeera.[33] Al Jazeera operates out of Qatar which is located in the Persian Gulf. The station aspires to be the CNN of the Arab world and uses a very Western style of reporting which is probably one of the reasons it has become so popular among the Arab public. Although it is difficult to know the exact size of its audience, the station apparently reaches tens of millions of people in that part of the world.

There has been a lot of criticism of Al-Jazeera in the United States because it is seen as an anti-American station, especially in its coverage of the Iraq War and the fact that Osama Bin Laden likes to use it for sending his various messages. But it is hardly surprising that news from an Arab television station would look very different than news that is broadcast in the United States. This point will be even clearer in the next chapter that talks about why there is no such thing as "objective" news.

Significantly, some of the fiercest opponents of Al-Jazeera are Arab leaders who in the past were able to effectively control the flow of information to their people. Al-Jazeera frequently presents stories that criticize these Arab regimes and this explains why the news organizations' reporters have often been arrested or thrown out of certain countries. Studies show however that many Arabs find Al-Jazeera much more credible than their local stations that mostly present news that has been carefully filtered.[34]

There are also some extremely positive developments associated with stations such as Al-Jazeera. The domestic news media in many of these countries were historically channels of propaganda with nothing getting through that was not approved by the government. For the first time millions of Arabs are being exposed to Western voices and opinions they would have never been heard in the past. This includes not only U.S. and European leaders but even Israeli spokespeople who are interviewed on a regular basis. This is not to say that these people are not often asked hostile questions ("when are you going to stop killing children?"), but they do get to tell their story to a tremendously large audience that until recently was unavailable.

The long term question that nobody can answer is whether this and other technologies will have a long term impact on closed societies. Will women finally be allowed to drive, or maybe even vote in Saudi Arabia? Will the fact that Iranians get access to Twitter and Facebook lead to a more open society in the country? Will the Internet increase the chances of bringing true democracy to China? Most scholars who have studied this question hopes that all of these changes will take place, but nobody really knows.

Media and Peace

We move from considering the role of the news media in wars to a more pleasant topic: attempts to bring peace. To do so we will travel to Northern Ireland and to the Middle East. Taking this trip again illustrates once more that when the authorities lose control over the political environment, they lose control over the news.

The Northern Ireland conflict was long and bloody with numerous attempts to bring it to an end.[35] The roots of the conflict lay in the feeling of the Catholic minority that they were being constantly discriminated against by the Protestant majority. They demanded that Northern Ireland be reunited with the rest of Ireland while the Protestants insisted the area continue to be part of Great Britain. The violence was terrible and led to over 3,500 deaths between 1969 and 2001.[36]

There was a serious attempt to bring peace to the area in November of 1985 with the Anglo-Irish agreement. Leaders were unable at that time to mobilize a consensus and this accord was rejected by many of the Unionist (Protestant) political parties. In keeping with the PMP principle, this lack of agreement was reflected, amplified, and reinforced in the news media, especially in the Protestant newspapers who took a firm position against the accords.

The situation changed however when former U.S. Senator George Mitchell began a new round of negotiations in 1995.[37] Mitchell was able to bring almost all of the Unionist and Nationalist parties to sign the Belfast Peace agreement on Good Friday 1998. Mitchell had two major conditions for all of the parties involved in the negotiations. The first was that they must refrain from all acts of violence and the second was that there would be no leaks about the negotiations to the news media. Mitchell understood that unless he could maintain control over events and information he would be unable to reach an agreement.

When the negotiations were completed Mitchell had managed to mobilize a good deal of support from both sides of the fence. There was some opposition, but the vast majority of political parties were supportive. This consensus in turn led to enthusiastic support by the local news media.[38] One study looked at the editorials written about this peace process in the *Irish News* (considered a Catholic newspaper) and the *Belfast Telegraph* (Protestant) between 1997 and 1999.[39] In the *Irish News* there were a remarkable sixty-four editorials in support of the peace process, five that expressed ambivalence, and only one that was opposed. The *Belfast Telegraph* was equally biased in favor of peace: sixty-two editorials in favor, eighteen in the middle, and again only one opposed. Those opposed to the peace accords justifiably felt that their voices weren't being heard.

When all of the major political forces are pointing towards peace, it doesn't mean they are right but it does mean that the news media will point in the same direction. I conducted interviews with political leaders and journalists in Belfast in the spring of 1999 and many talked about the effects of this new consensus on media coverage. One of the newspaper reporters put it this way:

> The other thing I've noticed is that, well, the media, you know there was almost a discomfort of even using the term peace process for a long time because a lot of Unionists wouldn't accept it was a peace process, it was a surrender process, or an appeasement process. I feel more comfortable using it now because the Ulster Unionists have embraced it to a degree, and are starting to take ownership of the peace process. But up until 96, the Unionists saw the peace process as a conspiracy by the Republicans to lure them into a united Ireland.[40]

Once again, if you compare the failed attempt of 1985 to the successful one in 1998, you will realize that political change came *before* media change. These comments also remind us that as with wars, one of the reasons that reporters adopt a certain tone about political issues is that they prefer not to annoy their audience. Unlike the 1985 agreement, the more recent peace process was not considered controversial, so journalists felt little need for "balanced coverage." In the end, the agreement was submitted as a referendum to the people of Northern Ireland and received 71 percent support. While there are still sporadic acts of violence in that part of the world, no one can dispute that the peace agreement has led to a much better life for the people of Northern Ireland. There is good reason to believe that the news media in Northern Ireland played a role in bringing the agreement to fruition.

Now we move to the Middle East where if you expect the worst you will rarely be disappointed. Israel was involved in two peace processes in the early nineties one with the Palestinians ("the Oslo Process") and the other with Jordan. These two examples provide a further demonstration of why a leader's control over the political environment is the key factor in explaining how the media operate. Prime Minister Yitzhak Rabin's government had very little control over the political environment surrounding the Oslo process but a great deal of control over the negotiations with Jordan.[41]

The Oslo peace process was extremely controversial from the start. Rabin had decided to negotiate with Israel's arch enemy—Yasser Arafat—and to recognize the Palestinian Liberation Organization. Many in Israel still considered the PLO a terrorist organization and were extremely angry with the prime minister. This led to massive protests by the right wing in Israel who was fervently opposed to any compromise that would involve giving back land in the territories that had been conquered during the Six Day War in 1967. Many of these protests turned violent and it was clear the government was having a great deal of trouble keeping a lid on the amount and intensity of the protests.

Even worse, the Hamas and other Palestinian groups carried out a massive number of terrorist attacks in Israel in an attempt to derail the process of reconciliation with Israel. In the first five years after Oslo, 279 Israelis were killed.[42] The level of internal political violence also continued to rise during the Oslo negotiations. On November 4, 1995, Prime Minister Rabin was assassinated by a right wing fanatic whose goal was to stop the Oslo peace process.[43] The Oslo peace process did eventually collapse and the Israeli-Palestinian conflict deteriorated even further with increasingly horrible levels of death and destruction on both sides.

So what was the role of the Israeli news media in all this? It would be both foolish and wrong to suggest that the Oslo peace process fell apart *because* of the way the press covered it. The process was flawed from the beginning. The fact that neither Rabin nor Arafat could take control over the violence or mobilize any consensus in their societies for the process provide far better explanations of why Oslo failed than anything having to do with media coverage. Many would also argue that given the scope of concessions each side would have to make in order to reach an agreement Oslo was doomed from the start. Once again, the argument is that if you want to understand what happens in the coverage of peace or war look at politics first.

On the other hand, the Israeli press was an important catalyst for accelerating the downhill spiral. A content analysis of Israeli newspaper coverage revealed that during the first 250 days of the process there was far more negative news about Oslo than positive.[44] This is hardly surprising given the huge number of negative events that occurred during this period. It is also worth noting however, that the analysis revealed that good things that were happening on the ground received very little attention. Conflict and violence are always considered more newsworthy than peace. Peace negotiations are pretty boring to cover and even if something interesting *is* taking place in the negotiations leaders from both sides have an interest in keeping it secret. In addition, research on the topic shows that a good deal of the coverage of the internal debate over Oslo and of the terrorist attacks was extremely sensationalist. This type of coverage tends to add fuel to the flames of conflict.

The Israeli peace process with Jordan, on the other hand, was the exact opposite of what happened during the Oslo accords.[45] Here Prime Minister Rabin was able to maintain control over events, the flow of information, and enjoyed an extremely large amount of consensus in support of the process. The reasons were that Jordan was always considered one of the most moderate of Arab countries, King Hussein was considered a positive personality, and the issues that divided the two sides were relatively small. There were no protests against the agreement and no acts of violence. Because the negotiations were cordial there were also virtually no leaks that could have threatened the talks. The extremely high degree of political consensus can be demonstrated by looking at the vote in the Israeli parliament (the Knesset): 105 in favor of the peace treaty with Jordan and only 3 against.[46] The only time any bill gets that type of support is when legislators are voting in favor of Mother's Day.

The final agreement between Israel and Jordan was signed on October 24, 1994. The Israeli news media was in full celebration mode with doves and flags prominently placed on the front page of the most popular newspapers.[47] The signing ceremony attended by President Clinton, King Hussein, and Prime Minister Rabin was held at 1:00 in the afternoon in the Arava desert. Those who know something about the desert might wonder why anybody in their right mind would have a ceremony in the middle of the afternoon. The answer is that because of the time difference this allowed Clinton to appear on the morning news programs in the United States.[48]

The point to remember from all this is that the importance of political control has as much to do with how the news media cover peaces as it does with how they cover wars. In fact the principle will also help you understand the role of the news media in any debate whether it be about health care, religion in the schools, or what should be done about global warming. If you keep your eye on how well the government is doing politically, you'll have no problem predicting how the media will cover the issue.

Spin Can Only Take You so Far

There was a movie produced a few years ago called *Wag the Dog* starring Dustin Hoffman and Robert Di Niro. It was a political comedy, and the idea was that because the president was involved in a sex scandal his spin doctors recommend that he manufacture an imaginary war with Albania to distract public attention. The drama is enhanced by the Albanians taking an American P.O.W. by the name of Sgt. William Schumann. One of the best parts of the film is when Willie

Nelson (yes *that* Willie Nelson) writes and performs a song called "Good Old Shoe" in support of the prisoner. The advisors then organize a "shoe throwing campaign" where Americans show their support by hanging their old shoes on lampposts and telephone wires. It is pretty clear that because of the news story the president was going to be reelected.

It was a good movie, but it perpetuates a myth about the power of spin. The myth is that there are powerful spin doctors that can take events and manipulate them in such a ways that they can turn any political disaster into a success story. One more understanding you should take away from this chapter is that such claims are, for the most part, nonsense. It is true that political power brings important advantages in selling one's story and that sometimes leaders who find a clever way of telling their story (e.g., calling it abuse rather than torture) can lower somewhat the amount of public damage. But in the final analysis, only political success brings true media success.

The extent to which genuine political success is an important condition for media success should be clear from the cases that were discussed. The fact that the first President Bush was able to mobilize a massive amount of national and international support for using force against Saddam Hussein meant that he had little trouble getting his message through to the news media (including the foreign news media). The Gulf War itself was short and successful. His son, on the other hand, started out with a great deal of support, but lost it as the war dragged on. In the end, it became clear to most Americans that the war had been a mistake and the United States had to find a way to extricate itself from the Iraqi quagmire. Similarly, the fact that Rabin was unable to prevent terrorist attacks or to mobilize a large coalition in favor of the Oslo process provided him with very little control over the Israeli media. The peace process with Jordan, on the other hand, had a lot in common with the American victory in the Gulf War: it was short, well executed, and ultimately successful.

The upshot of this idea is that spin can only take you so far. In the end, it is almost always the political dog wagging the media tail. This does not mean that the news media are simply passive conveyer belts passing everything they see and hear onto the public. Journalists have their own interests and routines and this has a major impact on how they construct news stories. The next two chapters are intended to bring you up to speed on the next part of the process.

Questions for Thought and Discussion

1. The relationship between journalists and the military during war time can be very tense. On the one hand, journalists claim that the public has the right to know what is happening on the battlefield, while military leaders believe that too much openness can endanger the troops and lower public morale. How much freedom should journalists have in covering wars as they see fit? Do you think the idea of having embedded journalist makes sense? Why or why not?

2. Many people believe that the technological changes in the way information is gathered and distributed has had led to significant changes in the political world. Can you think of any examples of political events or stories that would either not have been possible or would have had different results before the advent of the Internet? What types of political information do you receive through the Internet that you cannot get from the traditional news media?

Section II

Turning Politics Into News

In this section of the book the discussion moves from looking at the political actors' perspective to the news media perspective. The media do not merely reflect what is happening in the political world, they transform it into a product called news. This transformation follows certain norms and rules that ensure, among other things, as large an audience as possible. Once you understand these rules you will have a much better understanding about both what gets covered and how it gets covered. It is true that the range of initial ingredients for creating a news story depends almost entirely on what's happening in the political world. After that though it is up to the reporters and editors to decide which ingredients to use, which types of spices to add, and how to combine and prepare them so the final dish will attract and please their customers.

Chapter 3 is devoted to explaining why there is no such thing as objective news and why such a goal is impossible. The very fact that editors routinely search for news in a limited number of places and that they can only produce a limited number of stories every day tells you that journalists have to make difficult decisions about what to include and what to leave out. One of the most important factors in determining which events get selected has to do with what will be called *cultural bias*. People everywhere are most interested in events that concern them or their country, so it is quite understandable that journalists would give preference to stories that reflect this bias.

Cultural bias doesn't however just influence which stories make it through the editing process it also has a major impact on how these news stories are constructed. Journalists and their audiences all share certain assumptions about the political world, and, although most people don't think about them, these assumptions provide a basis for almost everything they get from the news.

When people usually talk about the lack of objectivity in the news, they are talking about something completely different. They are talking about *ideological bias*. The conventional wisdom is that most journalists are liberals who employ a leftist slant to every news story. These charges became especially pronounced in the 2008 election where there was a widespread belief that journalists were doing all they could to get Barack Obama elected. There is quite a bit of research on this issue and this will also be discussed in Chapter 3.

Chapter 4 deals with another form of journalistic partiality: *commercial bias*. News is a business and dramatic stories insure a bigger audience. The pejorative name that has been given to this tendency is *infotainment*. Many critics believe that as the news media become more sensational they lowered the level of public discussion and debate about the major issues facing the country. Returning to the food metaphor, selling cheap junk food will often increase profits but can have a terrible effect on people's health. Although most people don't relate to the emphasis on entertainment as a type of bias, it too determines which stories are selected, how much time and space they will be given, how they will be packaged and sold.

So in this section we move to the second part of the political communication process. After all, the political actors have had their say and after all the unplanned events have taken place it is up to the journalists to create this very special product known as news.

3   No Such Thing as Objective News

If one had to choose the single issue that bugs most people about the news, it is probably the issue of bias. The most common assumption is that journalists are all bleeding-heart liberals who continually refuse to give conservatives equal time. This belief provides at least a partial explanation for the establishment of a slew of conservative talk shows and for the creation of Fox News that claims without a bit of irony that it presents "Fair and Balanced News." There are also critics from the left who claim that the media are capitalist tools whose major interest is to protect elite interests.

There are many problems in deciding just what we mean when we talk about bias and even more when we try to measure it. This can be better understood by thinking about how most of us watch the news on television. Everything we agree with is obviously "true," so we don't pay much attention to it. Everything we disagree with is clearly biased. People are especially likely to see bias when they are emotionally involved in a conflict. Take, for example, a news story that appeared about Sarah Palin in July of 2010.[1] The former governor decided to weigh on the controversy concerning the plan to build a mosque near "Ground Zero" (the site of the 9/11 terrorist attack). She sent a tweet that said "Peaceful Muslims, pls refudiate." Unfortunately, refudiate is not a real word in English and this led to a feeding frenzy by the press. To make matters worse, when asked about it, Palin compared herself to Shakespeare saying that he too made up words.

If you look at the comments people made on the various news sites and blogs where this story was published, you get a pretty good idea of how people judge bias. Those that disliked Palin were thrilled that they had another opportunity to make fun of her. Those who admired the former vice-presidential nominee argued that this was further proof of the leftist bias of the news. Asking a person who is emotionally involved in a conflict about news bias makes about as much sense as asking a Boston Red Sox fan to umpire a game against the Yankees.

The third principle is stated like this: *There is no such thing as objective journalism (nor can there be)*. The real question is not, then, whether or not the media are biased (they are) the question is *how* are they biased. The discussion in this chapter will deal with two types of bias: cultural and ideological. Cultural bias has to do with the fact that every news story is rooted in a certain time and place. A news report about U.S. race relations in 1960 will look nothing like a report on the same topic in 2010. The issue will also look very different when it is reported in America, France, or Japan. One of the reasons why cultural bias is so powerful is that it is usually invisible. People are rarely called upon to question their basic assumptions about their world in part because ethnocentric news is so natural and familiar.

Ideological bias, on the other hand, appears much easier to recognize. It is certainly a major issue for public debate with countless columns and books ruthlessly attacking the news media for their slanted reporting. Fortunately, there is actually some good research on the question of ideological bias in the news. While none of these studies provide a final and definitive answer to this issue they do shed quite a bit of light on the topic.

Cultural Bias in the News

I'd like you to think about death for a few minutes. It is not a very nice thing to think about, but thinking about it provides an especially important insight about cultural bias in the news. In any given day there are thousands of people dying in ways that could be considered newsworthy. They are murdered, slaughtered, commit suicide, die in traffic accidents, perish in crashing planes and trains, killed in wars and terrorist attacks, die in natural and un-natural disasters, and expire in epidemics.

Almost none of these thousands of deaths will be reported in the news you get. Every news editor has to make decisions about what to cover and what to ignore. Television news is limited by the amount of broadcast minutes and newspapers by the number of pages. Even online news sites that have more space available are limited by the number of paid staff who can prepare stories and put them on the web. There is simply no room in the news for the vast majority of deaths that take place, especially those that occur in other countries. In other words, some deaths are more important to a particular audience than others. Local deaths are more newsworthy than deaths that happen far way and death from terrorism is far more interesting than deaths from traffic accidents.

News is, in the end, always local. Whether it is reporting about our city, our state, or our country the news tells us stories in ways that both interest and make sense to us as an audience. Every news medium in the world operates within a certain cultural context that is reflected in every news item that is produced. This is why many in the field of communication say that news is a "social construction." Every society has certain ways of looking at the political world and our news is constructed by taking those assumptions into account. What we are being fed goes down much easier that way.

The importance of these cultural considerations starts long before an editor decides whether or not to cover an event. The first question you need to ask is whether there are any Western journalists stationed in a particular place. Here's a way to remember this point: *News happens where there are journalists.* When an American newspaper decides to place most of its staff in the United States, a few staff members in Europe, and none in Africa it means there will be a steady flow of domestic news, some stories from Europe, and almost nothing from the invisible continent. Thus almost every American who follows the news has heard of President Nicolas Sarkozy (and many probably have also heard about his model/singer wife) but few could provide a single name of an African leader. It is true that many news outlets depend on wire services such as AP and UPI to provide them stories they can't get themselves, but even the wire services can't be everywhere.

The decisions made by news editors are based primarily on assumptions about what they assume their particular audience—and their potential audience—wants to hear about. This is just one reason why news could never be "objective." The very fact that editors have a very limited amount of space and that they make choices based on what interests their audience means that they are making subjective judgments all the time. People living in Atlanta have some interests they share with people living in Milwaukee (e.g. the president), but they also have local interests they only share with people living near them (their mayor). They have very few common interests with people living in Bucharest, Sidney, or Jakarta. So news from any of those places is unlikely to interest them. If one of those stories does come on television many see it is an excellent opportunity to make a sandwich.

If the American news media do take an interest in foreign countries, it is because the United States is directly involved. The Tyndall Report examines all of the news stories that appear on the national television networks on weekdays. In 2009, foreign stories accounted for 22 percent of news stories.[2] Now this may seem quite high, but looking closer one finds that by far the greatest number of foreign news stories had to do with conflicts where the United States was involved: the war in Afghanistan, then stories related to Iran, and then the Israeli-Palestinian conflict. Interestingly, the Iraq War was no longer in the top twenty. Not surprisingly, there were almost no stories about Latin America or Africa.

Another study that measured the amount of foreign news in 2009 was carried out in the Pew Project for Excellence in Journalism.[3] Looking at all different types of news media, the study found an average of ten percent of stories dealt with foreign topics not related to the United States. There were also some interesting differences between the media. Only 3 percent of all news stories on the cable networks dealt with foreign topics not related to the United States and a surprisingly high 17 percent of online news covered these topics. This last figure suggests that the new media may turn out to be less ethnocentric than the traditional press. The issue of how the new media deals with the world will be discussed below.

In any case, cultural bias does not only have an effect on which countries we hear about it also has an influence on *what* we hear about them. In general, when editors assume that their audience has little or no interest in a particular country, they will only cover it if something truly awful happens. Countries (e.g., Britain) that are considered important are covered on a regular basis and this means that routine events (elections, major speeches by the prime minister) get at least some exposure. The poorer countries are only covered when something extraordinary happens and those exceptions are almost always negative. It is sad but true that, from a news perspective, ten deaths in New York are worth about twenty-five in London, which are worth tens of thousands in Africa (and here too, only if they die all at once).

One of the consequences of this process is what can best be called the *principle of representative deviance*. If asked, people know that news deals with the deviant and unexpected. But if most of the information people get from the news is negative, few can resist coming to the logical conclusion that these stories provide an accurate description of the country. There is really no choice from most citizens: if that is all you hear your images of those countries will be negative.

If you want further proof of how this works, I'd ask you to think about the first thing that comes to your mind when you are asked to think about Indonesia? The first thing that is likely to be one of two things: either the tsunami that took place in 2004 or the terrorist attacks in 2003. There is never going to be any routine news coming out of countries like Indonesia so that is the way most Americans will think about these countries (if they ever think about them at all).

This constant flow of negative news about culturally distant countries brings us back to the distinction between front and back door coverage. The front door of respectable coverage is reserved for things that happen in either our country or countries we consider important. Weaker countries almost always enter through the back door because of some exceedingly deviant event. Ongoing negative coverage of these weaker nations in the Western news media is likely to lower any chances for investment or tourism in these countries. Here too then the news media become important agents for increasing the economic gap between the "haves" and the "have nots" only this time it takes place on an international scale.

One of the reasons why cultural bias can be so powerful is that it tends to be invisible. Most people who turn to the news media don't think about how little access they have to most of what happens in the world. Their view of the world is extremely narrow but unless somebody points it out, they are unlikely to notice. The way the news is constructed appears quite "natural" because this is the news we are used to.

News Frames

An excellent way to understand how cultural bias influences the way news stories are told is to think about *news frames*. The concept of frames came up earlier but this is a good time to go into more depth. News frames are organizing devices journalists use to tell a coherent story. You can think of it as an ongoing theme that runs throughout a particular story or a particular set of stories.

A good example would be the "War on Terror" frame that came into place after the September 11, 2001, attack in the United States. This phrase became an icon that appeared on every television screen in the United States and served to thematically link a variety of different news stories. This would include both stories about U.S. soldiers getting ready to leave for the War in Afghanistan and stories about what President Bush and everyone else in the world intended to do about the terrorist threat. The use of the War on Terror frame provides an important guide not only for audiences but also for editors, reporters, and camera operators.

Once a news frame has been established it serves two important functions for journalists. First, it operates like a powerful search engine as journalists go out in search for stories that fit the frame. Certain stories fit quite easily (the endless search for Osama bin Laden) while others don't (an Afghani wedding party accidentally getting bombed). Events that don't fit the frame are less likely to get much media attention. News frames are also tools for providing *meaning* to events. Once a news frame has been established, journalists use frames to tell us how to understand a particular event. In news stories connected with the War on Terror, for example, one finds heroes and villains as well as victories and defeats.

This explains why it was so important for the Bush administration to claim that the subsequent Iraq war was also part of the more general War or Terror. In this case, however, the Bush administration was less successful because certain people in the political elite, the news media, and many political organizations were unconvinced. Bush was unable to take control over the political environment surrounding the issue. Eventually, these groups received important support for their rejection of the War on Terror frame when government officials admitted that no real link had been found between Saddam Hussein and Al-Qaeda.

The fact that Bush was hoping to apply the War on Terror frame to the Iraqi War and others refused to accept it reminds us that political actors have their own *ideological frames* they are trying to promote. Think of these as packages of claims and ideas that are used to "sell" a particular viewpoint. When leaders and activists successfully promote their frames to the news media, it provides them with an enormous boost for their political efforts. Groups who want harsher laws against illegal immigration, for example, will often promote an "Anti-terrorist" frame arguing that such legislation would prevent terrorist from crossing the border.[4] More often than not, however, the news media find themselves dealing with *competing* frames. Those who want more liberal laws concerning immigration, for example, would try to frame the issue in terms of social justice.[5] In these cases, while journalists sometimes give certain frames preference, they may also decide to either give equal time to each frame or to construct their own.

Consider the controversial topic of abortion. There are two major camps and two major frames that are usually being promoted to the media and to the public: Pro-Life and Pro-Choice. Each group has chosen terms that culturally resonate with a large segment of society (who can be "anti-life?"). Each movement also has a package of terms and ideas that serve as rhetoric tools for convincing people that their positions should be accepted. The National Right to Life Organization provides the following abortion facts for people who come to their site.[6]

Heart begins to beat around 22 days from conception
There have been more than 40 million abortions since 1973

Women have cited 'social reasons,' not mother's health or rape/incest as
their motivation in approximately 93 percent of all abortions

A June 1999 Wirthlin poll found that 62 percent of Americans support
legal abortion in only three or fewer circumstances: when the preg-
nancy results from rape or incest or when it threatens the life of the
mother

The National Organization of Women, on the other hand, promotes a pro-
choice position. One of the strategies for promoting this frame is to talk about a
concept called "reproductive justice":[7]

Reproductive justice ensures that women are healthy, both physically and
emotionally; that they can make decisions about their bodies and sexual-
ity free from government interference; and that they have the economic
resources to plan their own families. A woman's well-being requires self-
determination, equality, and the respect and support of her society.

The goal of each of these groups is to speak to the news media and promote
their positions. Even better from their point of view would be if journalists were
to emphasize the group's preferred language and facts and to turn movement
leaders into routine sources. So this process brings us to the question of how
these contests play out in the news and which types of political actors are most
and least likely to succeed.

The Construction of News Frames

So how do the news media construct news frames? If anybody came up with
a simple answer to this question they'd be rich. After all, isn't this what public
relations is all about? While I hate to disagree with P.T. Barnum not all publicity
is good publicity. If the news media portray your organization as a bunch of
extremists, you will take a very serious hit in terms of contributions and volunteers
(and if you *do* suddenly get any new volunteers, you'd probably want to check
them for weapons).

Journalists construct news frames by trying to find a *narrative fit between
existing frames and the events they are covering*.[8] Journalists have a limited number
of interpretive frames on the social shelf and they take down the one that appears
to be the most appropriate for the events they are covering. As noted, when there
are competing frames (two or more frames on the shelf) they can either choose to
prefer one over the other or apply each to a different part of the story.

So the first step is to focus on what is on the shelf at a given time or place. The
available frames can only be understood by looking at the political, social, and
cultural environment in which the journalists are operating. William Gamson
and Andre Modigliani have a wonderful example of how important this can
be in understanding the construction of news frames.[9] Nuclear energy was first
developed in the United States immediately after World War II. It was seen as

a wonderful innovation with infinite potential and no serious risks. There was really only one frame that dominated both political discussions of the topic and in the media: progress. Nuclear energy was considered a positive development and one of the greatest inventions of all time.

This frame had important implications for how the news media covered nuclear plans. In 1966 there was a serious accident in the Fermi nuclear reactor which is located in Michigan: the cooling system failed and the fuel core had a partial meltdown. Because the dominant assumption was that nuclear power was safe, there was little news coverage of the incident. Gamson and Midigliani tell us that although journalists were informed about the accident almost nothing was reported. The *New York Times* took five weeks to report on the story and referred to it as a "mishap." This inattention meant that the political establishment had little reason to deal with the issue because nuclear energy was not seen as a serious threat to public safety.

Fast forward to 1979. At this point a significant number of movements had been active in promoting anti-nuclear frames. One of these was the "Runaway" frames that claimed that nuclear technology was spinning out of control and unless it was stopped disaster would result. As these challengers grew in influence, journalists began to understand that that there were now *competing* frames about nuclear energy: some in favor and some against. Political change (the issue had become controversial) had led to change in the media (more attention to the risks of nuclear power).

It isn't just the news media that reflect changes in the political environment, one will also find changes in books, television, films and (more recently) on the web. One of the most telling indicators of what happened at that time was a 1979 film entitled *The China Syndrome*. The movie, starring Jack Lemmon and Jane Fonda, tells the story of an accident in a nuclear plant in which the core becomes so hot it threatens to burn through the bottom of the plant. This type of meltdown and the subsequent radiation could kill thousands of people. The term *China Syndrome* refers to the fanciful idea that the core would keep burning through the center of the earth and eventually reach China.

In what can only be considered one of the most bizarre coincidences in history, twelve days after the film was released there was a partial nuclear meltdown in the Three Mile Island nuclear plant in Pennsylvania. This time the news media went crazy. The accident was a huge story and was published on the front page of every newspaper and led off the evening news for several days. Needless to say the movie *China Syndrome* turned into a blockbuster. More importantly the accident at Three Mile Island led to a complete change in policies concerning nuclear power in the United States; the number of nuclear reactors being built decreased dramatically and quite a large number of reactors were cancelled. It wasn't long before an even more horrible nuclear accident took place in Chernobyl, a city in the Ukraine. Chernobyl provided even more substantial evidence that nuclear power included serious risks. After Three Mile Island and Chernobyl, the Runaway frame became the most prominent frame in every form of media that was analyzed.[10]

We can learn quite a bit about news frames from the nuclear example. First, this is another excellent example of the Politics-Media-Politics cycle (PMP). In the early years of nuclear power the "Progress" frame was the only one available for journalists to use; there was nothing else on the shelf. It was only after anti-nuclear groups together with some political leaders started having success in promoting an alternative frame that the news began to talk about the "debate" over nuclear energy. The political environment in the United States (and other countries) had changed because nuclear energy had become a controversial issue. Once journalists recognized the controversy, they began giving more time and space to the anti-nuclear frame. This meant, at the very least, that many more Americans were being told about the possible risks of nuclear energy. The increased level of media attention also forces political leaders to take a stand on the issue; it is no longer something that can be ignored. This then is the second part of the PMP cycle: the change in media coverage leads to further political change.

Second, the example of nuclear energy also tells us that some events, especially major events, can provide important *advantages* to certain political actors and disadvantages for others. The reason a certain group gains an advantage is that one of the frames on the social shelf has a much better *fit* with current events than the other. The accidents at Three Mile Island and later in Chernobyl provided tremendous advantages to anti-nuclear groups attempting to make their case to the news media and the public.

The same dynamic of a particular group gaining advantages also happens when there is a particularly nasty environmental accident such as a train crash involving toxic waste. Green organizations suddenly have their phones ringing off the hook with calls from both journalists and volunteers. Chemical industry executives, on the other hand, are put on the defensive in news reports and pray for the wave (and the fumes) to quickly dissipate. Political waves are fickle however: they can run in different directions at different times. A dramatic rise in oil prices provides advantage to those favoring more off-shore drilling and for those who want to build more nuclear power plants. In fact this is exactly what happened when there was a major hike in oil prices in 2008. In 2010, however, the proponents of off-shore drilling faced a tidal wave of new critics because of the BP oil disaster, the biggest oil spill in U.S. history. The Republican chant of "drill baby drill" that seemed to resonate so well in 2008 had quickly become an embarrassing slogan to be avoided at all costs.

Most political events are more ambiguous in nature and do not provide clear advantages to any one frame. Take, for example, the decision by President Bush in 2007 to deploy 20,000 additional troops to Iraq. The move was named "The Surge."[11] Most Republicans supported the move and most Democrats—including Barack Obama—opposed it. The Republicans saw it as a way of achieving a certain amount of stability in that country (a "Stay the Course" frame) while the Democrats considered it a pointless effort to save a war effort that had gone terribly wrong ("Futile War"). The reactions of each side were predictable given the ongoing debate about the Iraq War. The initial decision to order a surge provided no clear advantage to either camp, and the U.S. news media provided each side with ample opportunities to present their views.

Over time, however, there was increasing evidence that the surge—together with other changes in policy—may have contributed to an increased level of stability in Iraq.[12] This explains why Senator John McCain was anxious to use his early support for the surge as proof that he was the better candidate for president. At that point in the election campaign, Senator Barack Obama did his best to avoid the issue. The increased stability in Iraq provided, at least temporarily, some advantages to the Stay the Course frame of the Iraq War. This is a case then of how an issue can begin without giving advantages to a particular frame, but, as time progresses, there is increasing evidence that one frame makes more sense than another. At that point the disadvantaged side is trying to duck under the wave while the advantaged side is attempting to ride the wave for as long as possible.

Returning to the nuclear energy example provides us with an additional lesson about news frames. When only one frame is allowed to dominate the news, it can be dangerous because other, potentially more sensible frames are ignored. A good example would be the "Deregulation Is Good" frame that was a common theme in economic news in the 1990s. Conventional wisdom held that the less the government intervened in the economy, the better it was for business. This consensus was reinforced by virtually every commentator that appeared in the media. Many now believe that this economic approach was one of the major causes for the economic meltdown that began in late 2008. Once again a major event provided important advantages to a pro-regulation counter-frame that had been ignored by the media before the crisis.

News frames are important because they can have a significant impact on public opinion and public policy. A perfect example can be found in a book by Frank Baumgartner, Suzanna DeBoef, and Amber Boydstun entitled *The Decline of the Death Penalty and the Discovery of Innocence*.[13] Surveys show that there has been a significant drop in public support for the death penalty in the United States. The authors make a convincing argument that one of the reasons is a significant change in the way the issue is being framed by both activists and the news media. Traditionally, debates over the death penalty were framed as either a moral issue ("an eye for an eye") or as a constitutional issue (cruel and unusual punishment). In the last few decades, argue the authors, there has been a much greater emphasis by the news media on an "Innocence" frame that claims that innocent people are being put to death. Not surprisingly, the increasing availability of DNA testing was one of the reasons for the growing resonance of this frame with the public. The most dramatic rise in the prominence of this frame took place in the nineties and coincided with, among other things, to the creation of the "Innocence Network" that now has offices in all fifty states.[14] There is also good reason to assume that changes in news frames may have been one of the reasons for a change in policies: several states declared a moratorium on use of the death penalty.

So, clearly, news frames matter. When political groups are able to find good evidence as well as supportive allies, the news media can change their approach to the issue. The death penalty example shows us how such changes in the media frames can be one of the forces that contribute to changes in the political process.

Friends and Enemies

News frames are also important for telling us about our national friends and enemies. This too is a form of cultural bias. Every news medium in every country in the world is inherently ethnocentric. Most Americans see the world in terms of four types of countries: friends, enemies, neutrals, and non-existent ("Is that really a country, or are you making it up?"). These cultural assumptions are then reflected in the way the news media frame the world. In general, our friends are noble and just and our enemies are horrible and cruel. It is true that allies can sometimes do bad things (France and Israel are good examples), but our enemies will almost never do anything good. See if you can find a U.S. news story in the last ten years that framed the President of Iran, Mahmoud Ahamadinejad in an even moderately positive light.

Robert Entman has a fascinating example of how such frames can be used to separate the good guys from the villains.[15] Two civilian airlines were shot down in the eighties. The first was a Korean Air Lines (KAL) plane shot down over the Soviet Union on September 1, 1983, killing 269 people, including dozens of Americans. The second was an Iranian plane that was shot down by a U.S. Navy ship on July 3, 1988, killing 290 people. In one case the enemy shot down a plane from a country allied with the United States and in the other the United States shot down an enemy's plane.

The reaction of the American press to these incidents was totally different and completely predictable. The first incident was framed as a case of murder in which the Soviets intentionally shot down a civilian plane. As Entman tells us, the headline in *Newsweek* after the incident was typical: "Murder in the Air." When, on the other hand, the United States shot down the Iranian plane, it was framed as a "technical glitch." The overall theme of the Iranian plane stories was that the plane being shot down was an unfortunate accident. In both case these frames were being promoted by the president and the State Department and adopted by the U.S. media.

Without going into the technical details about each incident, it is fair to say that there is no compelling evidence that either country purposely intended to shoot down a civilian airplane. The fact that such similar incidents could be explained so differently provides an important illustration of the ethnocentrism of news. Each story was shaped to meet American assumptions about the world.

Here's a good way to understand why journalists usually construct culturally biased news frames. There are four major questions you should ask about how any news story is constructed: (1) Who are the journalists who are responsible for creating the story? (2) Who are the major sources they use to gather information for the story? (3) What is the most important audience for the story? (4) What is the political context surrounding the issue when the story was constructed? Let's take each question in turn and show why it leads to a culturally biased view of the world using the two downed planes as an example.

When asking "who are the journalists," we need to think about their national, geographic, and ethnic background. The very fact that a journalist is American, French, or Indian will have a major influence on how they see and report about the world. Next time you watch the news on television try to count the number of non-Americans you see as anchors or reporters.[16] Unless you are watching an international news channel, the answer will probably be zero. Despite their often cynical view of politics, almost all journalists feel loyal to their country. When Americans are killed, it is understandably considered a tragic news story. When people are killed in another country, especially one that isn't considered important, the story will get much less attention and the victims less sympathy. Virtually all of the journalists who were covering the downing of the two planes were Americans and this, clearly, had a major influence on their perspective.

A second reason why stories are culturally biased is that they depend almost exclusively on American sources to find out what happened. This is especially true when it comes to quick-breaking international stories such as a plane being shot down. The only people who can quickly give reporters the information they need are at the Pentagon, the White House, and the State Department. It is also much easier to get them on the phone, because reporters call the same phone numbers on a regular basis. You can assume that when the Korean airline was shot down, it would have been much more difficult to get the Soviet Minister of Transportation on the phone (first you have to find if there *is* such a thing, then you have to find the country code for Russia, then you have to find someone who speaks English, then…).

When American officials talk to journalists they don't merely pass on information, they also attempt to explain what happened. In other words, they *frame* the events. This grants these officials tremendous power in promoting their world view to the U.S. media. While the advent of the Internet has made it easier for journalists to get access to foreign sources for information, there is little evidence that this has seriously altered their preference for their own official voices.

Once we turn to the third question—having to do with the nature of the audience—the picture becomes even clearer. Not only do we have American journalists talking to almost exclusively American sources, but they are constructing news that is designed for an American audience. The reason the traditional news media are called the "mainstream" media is because most news companies attempt to appeal to mainstream America. It is true that audiences in some parts of the county are less ethnocentric in their world view, but even they won't tolerate an overly sympathetic picture of enemies.

The fourth and final framing question deals with the influence of political context on news stories. One way to think about this is to say that *every political story starts in the middle*. When journalists construct political news stories, they almost never start with a blank slate. The vast majority of their audience already recognizes the major actors and can separate the good guys (friends) from the villains (enemies). In this sense most political news can be seen as an ongoing dramatic series to which people tune in to see what happens next. There is an occasional "special" when either a natural disaster takes place or a completely new candidate for president emerges, but even here journalists and audiences have a pretty good idea what to expect. The truth is that most news is not really that new.

The political context of the downing of the two planes is crystal clear: both of the other countries involved in the first incident were, at the time, considered enemies of the United States. When the KAL plane was downed in September of 1983, Ronald Regan was president of the United States and the Cold War with the Soviet Union was in full force. In fact, Reagan had dubbed the Soviet Union the "evil empire" only a few months earlier (March, 1983).

It is important to remember that allies can become enemies and enemies sometimes become allies. During World War II the Soviet Union was seen as an important U.S. ally against Nazi Germany, and the fact that it was a communist country didn't seem to matter much. Once the Cold War began, however, communism became a *very* big deal, and the rivalry between the two Super Powers continued for decades including the period when the KAL plane was downed. Relations between the two countries improved dramatically during the eighties and nineties with the fall of communism, the breakup of the Soviet Union, and Russia becoming somewhat more democratic. All of these changes were clearly reflected and reinforced in the way the American press covered Russia. In recent years tensions between the United States and Russia have again risen, and this too has been reflected in the way the U.S. leadership, the press, and the public relate to that country.

The bottom line is that the news media are important agents for constantly reminding us of why we hate our enemies. This was true when the Soviet Union was the major rival of the United States and no less accurate now that Iran and Islamic terrorists are enemies. Here too one can find the same patterns in television shows, movies, and novels. The villains in these plots are almost always chosen to reflect the prevailing political climate at the time. The same is true of the way the domestic news media in all countries cover the world, especially if they are involved in ongoing conflicts. There are a few exceptions to this rule and the domestic news media will sometimes show sympathy for victims on the other side. But such exceptions are extremely rare. Once the political leadership in a given country has defined a particular group or country as enemies, the news media's major concern is to understand the nature of that threat and what is being done to stop it.

Who You Calling a Deviant?

News frames do not only provide important information about foreign friends and enemies; they also reinforce and magnify people's beliefs about "deviant" and "extremist" groups within our own country. I put these words in quotation marks because social definitions about what is considered deviant also vary over time and place. Women's groups demanding the right to vote were once considered radical extremists. Here too, journalists do not just make this stuff up; they construct frames based on what they hear from their sources and those around them. In keeping with the PMP principle, when beliefs about these groups change—for better or for worse—so do news frames.

Minorities are often the ones that suffer the most from this inherent bias. For many years almost all U.S. journalists were White, their sources were White, their intended audiences were White, and the political climate was such that Blacks were seen as threats to the White majority.[17] This type of news coverage was everywhere including the supposedly liberal *New York Times*. As pointed out by commentator David Mills, one of the stranger themes in those news stories had to do with attacks by "Giant Negroes."[18] Headlines include: "Armed Negro Giant Goes Mad on Liner" (May 15, 1916), "Giant Negro Disables 4 Policemen in Fight" (June 12, 1927), and "Posse in Gun Battle Ends Giant Negro's Reign of Terror..." (March 6, 1932).[19]

Most would agree that news coverage of minorities in the United States is much less insulting in the twenty-first century. If we use the four framing questions that were formulated earlier, we get a better understanding of how these changes came about. As a reminder, the questions had to do with who constructs the stories, who their sources are, who the audience is, and what the political context is at the time the story is being produced. There are more journalists who are people of color than in the past, more minority sources, news stories are more likely to be written for a more ethnically diverse audience, and, perhaps most important of all, the political context concerning minorities has changed dramatically in the last fifty years. When one combines the impact of all four of these changes, one begins to understand why news about minorities is so different than in the past.

Once again, there are good reasons to believe that news media not only reflected the rise in Black status and power, but that they were also important agents in *accelerating* that process. Having leaders such as Colin Powell and Condoleezza Rice appear in the news on a regular basis no doubt paved the way for something that many thought impossible: a Black president. There are those who say that the first Black president was really David Palmer from the TV show *24* (while others claim it was Bill Clinton). Let's also not forget President Tim Beck who was played by Morgan Freeman in the movie *Deep Impact* (1998). Here too, the fact that television and movie executives were willing to produce movies and television shows with a Black president provides an important sign that public opinion about this issue had gone through a significant change. The same can be said with regard to changes in social attitudes towards homosexuality. Producing a show like *Ellen* in the nineties, which featured an openly lesbian actress playing a lesbian character, would simply not have been possible ten years earlier.

In each of these cases, the news media not only reflected the change in the public climate, they also sent an important message to everyone that this is how people *should* relate to the issue. Political tolerance is in and intolerance is out.

The fact that this change in climate is repeatedly expressed and amplified in both the news and entertainment media not only has an influence on how people see this issue, but it also influences the way political leaders speak about the topic.

One of the most successful ways for the news media to define political deviants is to simply ignore them. Here's a good example. In addition to the Republicans and the Democrats, twelve political parties put up a candidate for president in 2008. Try to name just three of them. I will give you the answer in a minute, but first I need to make a point. The reason why you are having so much trouble is that the news media saw no reason to cover these parties. These parties are ignored because they are considered as either unimportant, extremist, or both. The last time small parties that received any serious coverage was when Ralph Nader ran in 2000 as head of the Green party (yes, that is one of the parties that put up a candidate in 2008) and especially in 1992 when Ross Perot ran as head of the Reform party (yet another from 2008).

If the news media were truly "objective" or even "fair," then they should provide equal coverage to all political parties, even those that don't have a chance of being elected. If you consider that extreme, shouldn't they be given *some* time to present their views? But when most people talk about "balanced" news they are talking about giving equal time to Democrats and Republicans. Here then is the list of small parties that ran in 2008: Constitution Party, Green Party, Libertarian Party, Independent Party, America's Third Party, Boston Tea Party, New American Independent Party, Prohibition Party, Reform Party, Party for Socialism and Liberation, Socialist Party USA, and the Socialist Workers Party.

To find out anything about these political parties—or the dozens of independent and write-in candidates who ran with no political party at all—one would have to go out and search alternative sites on the web. This is a good demonstration, by the way, of why one should be skeptical of those who oversell the power of alternative news sites to change the political world. Each of these political parties had a web site and many received some coverage on alternative news sites. None of this, however, brought them any closer to having an effect on the national, state, or even local elections. The mainstream news media ignore these political parties because journalists see them as marginal and in doing so guarantee that those parties stay that way.

When less mainstream political groups do get news coverage, the mass media have an alternative way of marginalizing them: through labels. Here are some framing terms you should look for when reading or viewing the news: "violent," "extremist," "radical," "fringe," "fanatical," "communist," "socialist," "fundamentalists," "zealots," "cult," or (one of the best) "suspected of having ties to Al-Qaeda." If a group manages to get away with only being called "wacky," "weird," or "bizarre," they should consider themselves lucky. Sometimes these labels are used by the journalists but more often they appear in news stories as quotes from politicians, government officials, or people in the military or the police. In addition, in keeping with the notion of back-door coverage, when the spokespeople from such groups are quoted, it will usually be the weirdest or scariest quotes that are used.

Now all this is not meant to suggest that some of these groups, or even most of them, do not deserve these labels. There are some dangerous groups out there, and if the mainstream media makes it more difficult for evil to survive and flourish, that's fine. The point is that these labels are often based on the news media relying too heavily on official perspectives, the need to create drama, or because journalists tend to conform to the mainstream views of their audience. When you watch or read the news you need to always ask yourself whether *you* believe the labels are justified. This, of course, is not an easy thing to do because almost all of your information comes from the media. It never hurts, therefore, to also turn to some alternative news sites to get a different perspective. It is also worth repeating that such labels can prove to be transitory. Those who fought for civil rights, women's rights, gay rights, and those who opposed either the Vietnam or Iraq wars were all labeled radicals when they began their struggle. Eventually, it was often those who opposed these ideas who found themselves in the minority.

The New Media and Cultural Bias

What about the "new" media? Do they present a less ethnocentric view of the world? To put it differently: Do Internet sites, blogs, and other alternative sources of political information present a wider, more cosmopolitan view of the world? As with many issues concerning the new technology, there isn't enough good research to come to a firm conclusion about this issue. The initial conclusions are mixed.

First the good news. When it comes to having *access* to international news, it is indeed a whole new world. Those who have an interest in foreign countries can find news in almost any language, including news that has been prepared and edited by journalists living in each country. Even those who only speak English are only a click or two away from finding out what is happening almost anywhere of the world (especially as the instant translations improve). Equally important, the events are reported in real time so those who care about international affairs can remain completely up to date.

In addition, as was mentioned before, the initial findings suggest that online news has significantly more international news than the traditional news media. This is important because according to the Pew Research center as of 2009 61 percent of Americans get some news online.[20] This puts online sources behind only television as a source of news and ahead of newspapers.

This finding suggests that as the number of online news users rises, more people will be exposed to international news. There is however a second question. How much is this news *truly* international. How much are the stories constructed in ways that are very different than most Americans are used to see. Are those who turn to online sources also seeing events being framed differently?

Those who have studied the new media are not overly impressed by their diversity. Chris Patterson has done quite a bit of research on the topic and convincingly argues that many online news sites give more of an *illusion* of diversity than actual diversity.[21] The most important reason for this is that almost all of these sites depend on four news agencies for reporting on international affairs: Reuters, AP, BBC, and Agence France Press (AFP). There are, of course, exceptions to this rule—such as CNN and the *New York Times*—but for the vast majority of news organizations it just doesn't make any economic sense to have reporters roaming the world collecting information. It turns out that outsourcing is just as important for constructing international news as it is for constructing cars.

As Patterson points out, one of the more bizarre consequences of this is that when readers are offered hundreds of links about a news story, those who click on them end up mostly reading the same story. When almost every news site depends on the same news agencies, it really doesn't matter much whether citizens get it from Yahoo.com, the online versions of the *Chicago Tribune,* or even a Canadian online news site such as the *Calgary Sun.* This is what Patterson means by the illusion of diversity.

But perhaps this is not really such a big problem. If the news agencies are producing content that provides a broader perspective on the world and more people are being exposed to these stories, then this should lower the level of cultural bias in the news. There are reasons to believe however that this is not what is actually happening.

First, when it comes to the type of news stories produced by the news agencies, they prepare them with their most important clients in mind. As in any business, this usually means appealing to their wealthiest customers which in this case are the United States and Europe. Here's the way Patterson put it:

> Because news agencies must please all news editors, everywhere, they must work harder than their client journalists to create the appearance of objectivity and neutrality. In so doing, they manufacture a bland and homogeneous, but still ideologically distinctive, view of the world; stories challenging the ideological positions of the dominant political players on the world scene (in agency eyes, the US and UK) receive little attention.[22]

So even when it comes to the online news world, political power can often be translated into power over the media. This principle also works when we are talking about international political power. If you think for a second about the world of television and films, this is just as true in the entertainment world as it is in news. *American Idol* is shown in a huge number of countries, but television shows produced in other countries are forced to rely on either their local audience or audiences from other nations who speak the same language. There aren't many countries where the 2009 hit *Avatar* was not shown, but how many foreign movies do *you* watch in a given year?

The second reason why online news may not be more multicultural than other forms of news has to do with editorial discretion. News agencies such as Reuters and AP do provide online news editors with quite a few international news stories to choose from. But most online news sites also have to cater to their audience and including too much "foreign" news could drive people away.

There's a small experiment you can carry out to demonstrate this point (don't worry, no electric shocks are involved). First, go to your computer (you should probably take the book with you). Now go to any of the major online sites where most people see the news. You can either go to major portals such as Yahoo or MSN or online versions of either a local or national newspaper (such as *USA Today*). Once you are on the home page, try to get a sense of the proportion of the international news to national news on the page. This is the information that is being "pushed" at you every time you log on to one of these sites. The international stories you do find on this "front page" will mostly come from either a major international player, a well-known enemy of the United States, or some type of disaster. It is true that most of these online news sites also have a link or a tab called something like the "World," which will provide international news stories to those that are interested. In this case the more interested citizens are "pulling" international information from these sites, in other words actively searching.

One can certainly argue that a simple click brings you far more international news than you would have ever gotten from the traditional news media. Those who want to make the extra effort can carry out a series of clicks and will have access to almost every corner of the world. But now take a closer look at this international news and ask yourself two questions: (1) Did it come from one of the Western news agencies mentioned above? (2) Is there anything in the piece that sounds strange, offensive, or inappropriate for an American audience (e.g., positive coverage of Iran or Northern Korea or coverage of a country you've never heard of)? The answer to the first question is probably yes and the answer to the second will most likely be no.

Now, if you want to become a serious researcher, go one step further. Take a look at a news site that *originates* in a different country. Go, for example, to the *Times of India* (http://timesofindia.indiatimes.com/). Only now you are starting to see a very different type of news. It is true that here too one will find quite a few news stories that come from those news agencies as well as news about the United States. Due to previously mentioned differences in international power, Indian journalists are far more interested in the United States than American journalists are in India. But you are also seeing a very different set of news stories not only from India, but from countries that matter to India such as Pakistan and China. There will also be more news about Bollywood and, if you really want, you can also read some fascinating news about cricket. Looking closer you will find that it is not just the list of topics that is different, it is also the way the stories are written. They are written by Indian journalists using mostly Indian sources and writing for an Indian audience. You'll also find a similar Indian-centered approach to events if you read the blogs that originate in that country.

In summary, examining the content of the news media does suggest that the technological changes that have taken place may indeed provide more and easier access to international news. In addition, the fact that people need less effort (a click or two) to get to international news may lead more people to explore other places and viewpoints. It is too early to know whether this trend will continue. One thing I have learned as a social scientist is that I only make predictions about the *past* (and even those I don't always get right).

Ideological Bias in the News

So now, finally, we get to the major question that interests most people: the questions of ideological bias. Most political activists accuse the mainstream media of bias but, not surprisingly, they don't agree on the direction. Conservatives believe that the media slant dramatically towards the liberal side of the spectrum while liberals think the media promote conservative and big-business values. In fact the truth is much more complex than suggested by either of these shallow perspectives.

It is perhaps helpful to start by stating what is generally meant when people talk about liberalism and conservatism.[23] Although such categorizations are always problematic, one way to summarize the differences is to talk about how liberals and conservatives relate to the role of government in our lives. Liberals believe that citizens should be collectively responsible for each other's welfare. This means, among other things, that the government is expected to actively intervene with policies that help the less fortunate members of society. This underlying belief often translates into a "bigger" government. Liberals tend to support policies such as universal health coverage, affirmative action, feminism, and the regulation of the financial institutions. Conservatives believe that individuals should be responsible for their own welfare and the government should stay out of people's lives as much as possible. It is assumed that when people act in their own interests, society benefits. Conservatives are against gun control, against affirmative action, and in favor of lower taxes and a free market. In addition, liberals and conservatives differ with regard to the place of religion and tradition in society. Conservatives are more support of religious values, which explains why they are Pro-Life and want less separation between church and state. Liberals are generally Pro-Choice and oppose any religion in the schools.

Those who write popular books on the topic of media bias usually provide the most simplistic approach to this issue. They simply take one side or the other in this argument and write with passion using a large number of examples to "prove" the case. These books also have great titles that talk about "lies," "the *real* story," or the "idiots" on the other side. If you were to read just one of these books, you would probably be totally convinced that the author was right on the mark about media bias. When one is confronted with so much "compelling" evidence of news coverage that clearly tilts in one direction or another, how can one not come away convinced? If, however, you decide to read a number of books from different camps one of two things will probably happen. Either you will be convinced by those who are closest to your own opinion or you will be left confused (and go back to either reading fiction, watching television, or spending even more time on Facebook).

The problem with such books is that they are based on anecdotal evidence. I should mention that the word *anecdotal* is considered an especially vulgar profanity among most social scientists. The problem with anecdotal evidence is that if you look hard enough you can usually find what you're looking for. All you have to do is scan thousands of hours of television news, listen to hours upon hours of talk radio, read thousands of pages of different newspapers, and ignore any examples that disprove your point. In fact this description is perhaps overly flattering. Most pundits probably don't really spend thousands of hours gathering the "evidence" (let's hope they at least spend *hundreds* of hours).

One of the first significant studies of media bias was a book entitled *The Media Elite* written by S. Robert Lichter, Stanley Rothman, and Linda Lichter.[24] Their study tried to understand the level of liberalism in the press by looking at the political views based on a relatively large survey of journalists. Their conclusions, which are often quoted by conservative groups, was that most journalists were urban, nonreligious, and liberal. Fifty-Four percent of the journalists described their views as left of center, twenty-nine percent as "middle of the road" and only 20 percent reported being on the right. This was very different than what was found in the broad public where at the time there were more people describing themselves as conservatives than liberals. The researchers also found that the journalists were far more likely to vote for Democratic candidates for president than Republicans.

Activists on the left, on the other hand, are much more likely to quote the results of a 1998 study carried by the liberal organization Fairness and Accuracy in Reporting (FAIR).[25] One of the important points they made in the study was that when talking about the liberalism and conservatism of journalists one had to ask about their attitudes towards specific issues. Are we talking about liberalism with regard to social issues, foreign affairs, crime, the economy? They also carried out a survey of American journalists and compared this with the views of the general public based on national polls.

There was an interesting difference when one examined journalists' opinions on a number of political issues. The first thing to note is that most journalists described themselves as "centrists" on most issues. When asked about their opinion on specific issues some important distinctions emerged especially with regard to their views on "social" and "economic" issues. The social issues had to do with topics such as gay rights and abortion while economic issues were concerned with things such as whether or not employers should provide health care benefits or whether the there should be cuts to social security and Medicare benefits. The assumption with regard to economic issues was that liberals would want employers to pay for health and they would be against any cuts in government benefits. The study found that journalists were indeed more liberal in terms of social issues but were more conservative than the public with regard to economic topics. Even if some will be suspicious of the findings because the research was conducted by a liberal group, the study does remind us of the importance of clearly defining what we mean by a liberal bias. Ordinary citizens and journalists can certainly be liberal with regard to some issues and conservative with regards to other issues.

The question of how to *measure* liberal bias is even more difficult than the issue of how to define it (although, of course, the two questions are related). There are quite a few studies, for example, that take the approach described above by asking journalists about their views and then comparing those responses to those given by the general public.[26] A number of these studies have also come to the conclusion that journalists tend to be more liberal. The underlying assumption is that liberal journalists will generally construct liberal news stories.

There are a number of reasons, however, to question that assumption. First, neither the individual news organ nor the journalists themselves are interested in being identified with a particular camp because it will cost them serious money if they lose significant parts of their audience. Second, few journalists would give up a great news story just because it hurt liberals. Their professional reputation and advancement depends primarily on their ability to produce interesting news stories not advancing a candidate or cause. Third, journalists are extremely dependent on official sources. As discussed in the first chapter, the relative political power of these sources is likely to be far more important than the political views of the journalist. When conservatives are in power, they are far more likely to have routine access to the reporters than liberals who are in the opposition.

Some serious studies have tried to grapple with the issue of how to measure ideological bias. One of the most important is a "meta-analysis" carried out by Dave D'Alessio and Mike Allen.[27] A meta-analysis looks at all of the studies done on a research question and tries to come to an overall conclusion about what was found. The idea is that if many different studies using different approaches and methodologies come to the same conclusion they are more likely to reveal what is really going on. If you've ever used the Rotten Tomato web site to decide whether or not to go to a movie, you get the idea. D'Alessio and Allen examined a total of 59 studies and found no significant biases in newspapers and only an extremely small liberal bias in television news.

The results from individual studies, even when they are carried out by serious researchers are mixed. Tim Groseclose and Jeffrey Milyo decided to look at a wide range of American news media and at the amount to which each news medium cited liberal and conservative think tanks.[28] This provided them with the first measure of ideological bias. In the second stage, they compared the news content with the voting records of representatives in the House and the Senate on various issues. Based on this measure, they found most of the news media to be far to the left of most of the political leaders.

Another study carried out by Tawnya Covert and Philo Washburn used a completely different approach and came to a different conclusion.[29] They did a content analysis of coverage in *Time* and *Newsweek* of crime, the environment, gender, and poverty from 1995 to 2000. Then, they compared these results to the coverage in two clearly partisan magazines: the conservative *National Review* and the liberal *Progressive*. Finally, they calculated "bias scores" and concluded that the two magazines were "centrists." Some would argue that being centrist is also a form of bias, but for most critics the question is whether the media tilts towards the left or right.

One other major study worth citing is by David Niven in his book: *Tilt?: Search for Media Bias.*[30] Niven argues that one of the problems in measuring bias is that both pundits and researchers often find themselves covering events that are not really equivalent. In an election campaign, for example, one cannot talk about balance in the amount of coverage unless both candidates are equally newsworthy. This is unlikely to ever be the case, so the fact that one candidate receives much more news coverage does not mean the press is biased. It is worth adding that when one candidate or leader is more successful than another, the press cannot be blamed for covering it that way.

Niven examined differences in the tone of coverage when Democratic or Republican presidents found themselves with similar types of successes or failures. One example was how much credit or blame these leaders received when they found themselves facing the same level of unemployment. The logic of the study was that if the press is biased they should give one party's leader either better or worse coverage even thought the objective situation was the same. His careful analysis revealed absolutely no media bias in the coverage of these types of stories. In other words, news values are far more important than the ideological background of the journalists.

You begin to see the problem. Ideological bias is an extremely difficult thing to measure. Just as each pundit takes a different set of examples to prove a point, social scientists use different measures of bias. This reinforces why the meta-analysis is probably the best way to look at this issue. It would be nice if we could at least say with regard to ideological bias that "we know it when we see it"—as was said by Supreme Court Judge Potter Stewart in his attempt to define pornography—but we can't.

The Media is in the Tank for Barack Obama

In order to understand why ideological bias is so complicated, let's take what many consider the clearest case of political bias in the news media: the coverage of the 2008 election of Barack Obama. Almost everyone agrees that the U.S. press fell in love with Obama almost from the start.[31] The press support for Obama appears to have begun when he was running against Hillary Clinton and this affection appeared only to grow more passionate in the race against John McCain. This was the conventional wisdom, even among Democrats.

There was a wonderful routine about this bias on the notoriously liberal *Saturday Night Live* TV show during the primary race between Obama and Clinton.[32] The two candidates are having a debate, and the moderator asks the candidates some rather difficult knowledge questions. The bit goes like this:

Moderator: Senator Hillary Clinton. Nigeria's Foreign Affairs Minister can you name him?

Clinton: I, uh … don't know.
Moderator: Odo Madueke. Senator Obama, same question.
Obama: Odo Madueke.
Moderator: Correct! Senator Clinton, Sri Lanka's Deputy Ambassador to the
            U.N. Who is it?
Clinton: Oh, oh, it's Presad, uh, uh…
Moderator (interrupts): It's a trick question, that post is currently vacant. Senator
            Obama, same question.
Obama: I don't believe there is one at the moment.
Moderator: Correct!

There was another episode on *SNL* where the fawning correspondent's question to Obama is whether the senator is comfortable and whether he'd like a pillow. In an example of reality imitating fiction, Hillary Clinton referred to the routine in the next real debate between the two candidates. She was protesting the fact that she was always forced to answer the questions first and then added: "Maybe we should ask Barack if he's comfortable and needs another pillow."

As noted, there was also a widely-shared belief that the media was extremely biased for Barack Obama during election campaign against John McCain. In fact in a poll carried out by the highly respected Pew Research Center in October of 2008, 70 percent of Americans believed that the press was biased for Obama and only 9 percent thought the press favored McCain (the rest either thought the candidates were getting equal treatment or didn't give an opinion).[33]

The Pew Research Center also did a very serious content analysis of the news content of over 2,400 news stories from forty-eight news outlets during the six weeks from the end of the conventions through the final debate.[34] Both the results and their interpretation provide important evidence about the nature of bias in the press. The researchers found that the press didn't given an unusual amount of favorable coverage to Obama; it simply gave a disproportionate amount of negative coverage to McCain. In fact there were three times as many unfavorable news stories about McCain than there were positive ones. Obama, by contrast had a fairly similar amount of positive and negative stories written about him. So on the face of it, this should be the smoking gun: The U.S. press *was* in the tank for Barack Obama.

There is, however, one major problem with this conclusion. Was all the negative news about McCain because the journalists didn't want him to be president (assumedly because they don't like Republicans) or was it because there was simply much more negative news to report about the McCain's campaign? This brings us back to the earlier point: the more successful politicians will always get more favorable coverage. The Pew research shows, for example, the McCain coverage started positively but became sharply negative after his first reaction to the economic crisis (he said that the "fundamentals of our economy are strong"). McCain then suspended his campaign and returned to Washington, which to quite a few people seemed more of a campaign gimmick than a serious response to the crisis. Now add to that the fact that Obama was continually rising in the polls as McCain was dropping and you begin to ask: was there simply more bad news about McCain or did the press make a conscious or unconscious decision to report more bad news about McCain and less about Obama?

Here is the way the Pew report put it:

> One question likely to be posed is whether these findings provide evidence that the news media are pro-Obama. Is there some element in these numbers that reflects a rooting by journalists for Obama and against McCain, unconscious or otherwise? The data do not provide conclusive answers. They do offer a strong suggestion that winning in politics begat winning coverage, thanks in part to the relentless tendency of the press to frame its coverage of national elections as running narratives about the relative position of the candidates in the polls and internal tactical maneuvering to alter those positions. Obama's coverage was negative in tone when he was dropping in the polls, and became positive when he began to rise, and it was just so for McCain as well.[35]

Now this certainly sounds like a PMP cycle. Political change (McCain making mistakes and falling in the polls) leads to media change (more negative coverage of McCain) that probably led to further political change (fewer people willing to vote for McCain). As the Pew researchers put it by looking at the actual events, it would appear that the coverage can be better attributed to "reinforcing—rather than press generated effects of the media."[36]

The problem with this smoking gun is that Barack Obama had a lot of things going for him that had nothing to do with a liberal bias. He was simply a great news story. Here is the first Black man in the history of the country with a realistic chance to become president of the United States. He has an extremely charismatic personality, an amazing speaker, and someone who ran an almost flawless campaign. Huge and enthusiastic crowds greeted him not only in the United States but also abroad. From a news point of view Hillary Clinton was the first woman with a serious chance to become president, but she was already a well known personality. John McCain ran an extremely problematic campaign so the question which cannot be answered is whether the media would have covered him differently if his popularity had *risen* and Obama's had fallen during this time.[37]

The point is that there are many cases in which the ideological and commercial interests of the press push in the same direction, and this makes it impossible to sort out the "real" reason for bias. The best tests for liberal bias take place when these considerations run in *opposite directions,* cases in which the assumedly liberal news media finds themselves with an extremely popular conservative candidate or a major event that gives clear advantages to conservative arguments.

Here are some examples to consider. President Ronald Reagan was often called the "the Great Communicator" because of his ability to speak in ways that resonated with so many Americans. He was an extremely conservative leader but, in an important biography by Mark Hertsgaard, the author claimed that the supposedly liberal press was mostly a mouthpiece for the Reagan White House.[38] A second example would be the amazingly positive and enthusiastic coverage of George H.W. Bush during the first Gulf War.[39] As is often said, nothing succeeds like success. It is true that his popularity declined as the country's attention turned inward, but it certainly suggests that Republican presidents can achieve enthusiastically positive coverage. The same can be said about the extremely positive coverage George W. Bush received after the September 11, 2001, attacks.[40]

There are also other examples that suggest that commercial considerations are far more important than any ideological predilections. Consider, for example, the massive coverage of the Monica Lewinsky affair. Clinton was a very popular Democratic president, but the press devoted an enormous amount of time and space to this affair because it was such an incredibly juicy story. I think it would be fair to say that Democrats caught in good scandals are just as likely to be skewered by the media as Republicans. Here are two examples: New York Governor Eliot Spitzer who had to resign because he visited prostitutes and Governor Rod Blagojevich who was arrested and later impeached for allegedly trying to sell Barack Obama's Senate seat. These were both Democrats and yet the news and entertainment media turned each of these politicians into national jokes.

There is one more point that you should keep in mind when thinking about the supposedly liberal media. The news media love, more than anything else, conflict and war. In fact without conflict there wouldn't be much left to report apart from Brangelina and Koala bears coming to the local zoo. A truly liberal, dovish press would put much more emphasis on peace and reconciliation. But peace is simply not newsworthy. Imagine replacing the normally menacing music that marks the beginning of "Action News" with the Beatles song "All you Need is Love." It doesn't really work, does it? Peace and love make for great music but lousy news. There is a good reason for the adage: "if it bleeds it leads." The world portrayed by the news media is frightening, and this emphasis provides important advantages to those leaders who are promoting a tough stand against crime and a hawkish approach to foreign affairs.

So what's the bottom line? Based on the evidence, there is good reason to believe that most American journalists tend to be more liberal than the average American. It is also difficult to claim that this difference never has an influence on the way journalists cover politics, especially when it comes to social issues and human rights. Nevertheless, there is good reason to believe that cultural bias is a far more powerful influence on how news is constructed. Journalists and their audiences are both products of the social and political environment in which they live. In addition, the fact that the cultural filter is for the most part invisible makes it that much more effective. People are rarely forced to confront their most basic assumptions about the political world.

There is another filter employed by the news media that has been alluded to before and has a major impact on the construction of news: *commercial bias.* Commercial bias refers to the tendency of journalists to choose, highlight, and create dramatic news stories. Stay tuned because that's coming up next.

Questions for Thought and Discussion

1. There was a good deal of discussion in this chapter about the notion of frames. Find an example of a public debate that is going on in the news media. Try to give a title to at least two competing frames that are being promoted and think about the language or visual images antagonists are using (or should use) to promote their frames. Would you say that the media coverage is more sympathetic to one of the frames? Are there any interesting differences in how the debate is framed in various news media?

2. Do you think that most news media have a liberal or conservative bias? If you have an opinion about this issue, try to take the *opposite* position and see if you can find news stories that support that position. Now think about your actual opinion. How could you convince someone from the opposite camp that your claims about media bias are correct?

4　Telling a Good Story

The date was March 30, 2008. Senators Barack Obama and Hillary Clinton were involved in a knock-down drag-out fight for the Democratic Party nomination for president. When Obama woke up that morning, he didn't realize that it would turn out to be an extremely embarrassing day for him. He was traveling in Pennsylvania and making extra efforts to exhibit the "common" touch. Unfortunately, one of the ways he decided to do this was to go bowling. It was a disaster. His final score was a mere 37! Now to be fair, he only completed seven frames so perhaps his score would have improved somewhat in the end.

The Barack Obama bowling story quickly became big news. It was shown all over the country on television, radio, newspapers, and went viral on the Internet. There was quite a bit of discussion about how stupid he looked, and Hillary Clinton held a press conference on April Fool's day to suggest that the two candidates should have a bowling match to decide the election.[1] Humor aside, there can be little doubt that far more Americans knew Obama's bowling score than his platform on illegal immigration.

While many people seem convinced that reporters spend their time finding ways to manipulate public opinion, a journalist's first priority is to attract a large audience. While journalists also want to influence what happens in their community and their country, their greatest nightmare is to be scooped by the competition. In the digital age the importance of speed has become even more critical and this leaves reporters with little time to produce serious news. Hence, the fourth principle in making sense of media and politics: *The media are dedicated more than anything else to telling a good story and this can often have a major impact on the political process.*

However, every dramatized story does not have a major impact on the political process. There is no reason to believe that the Obama bowling story had any effect on the Pennsylvania primary (although he did lose that one). This is why the principle states that "this *can* often have a major impact on the political process." The impact of the obsessive search for drama is more like the cumulative effects of a steady diet of junk food rather than the impact of one specific meal.

It is worth taking a second to think about why we even call it a news "story." One reason is that anything reported on the news is expected to have all of the elements of a good story. It should have heroes and villains, conflict (especially bloody conflict), interesting characters, and above all a major dose of drama. Many news stories are also constructed as episodes in an ongoing series ("The War in Afghanistan," "The Struggle over Abortion," "Obama and Health Care Reform"). The best episodes need to be sufficiently gripping so that the audience feels compelled to come back and see how the story resolves. People like to hear stories and if they are "based on a true story" it makes them even more appealing.

There is a useful name for this that has become popular in recent years: *infotainment*. It is a derogatory term meant to suggest that the news isn't a serious means for informing the public; it is a simply another entertainment channel. There is quite a bit of truth to this claim, but not uniformly across all forms of news. Think of a continuum on which one finds the most sensationalist media at the one end and the most serious outlets at the other. At one end you find tabloid newspapers that seem to publish as much fiction as fact. Here one will also find what is sometimes referred to as "shock radio." Many of these programs resemble a lively bar where a bunch of inebriated—and yet surprisingly articulate—experts scream about the world. On the other end of the spectrum one finds understated newspapers such as the *New York Times*, the *Washington Post*, and the *London Guardian*. It is not that these "elite" newspapers go out and actively search for boring stories. They too want to find the most interesting news for their front pages. The difference is that the editors know their audiences are more interested in world affairs than whether Britney Spears has gained weight.

Despite these differences, drama is always one of the most important criteria for an event to be considered newsworthy. The emphasis on drama influences every stage in the editorial process: the selection of people and the events to cover, the types of questions journalists ask, the information that is collected and discarded, the photos and videos that are taken, the creation of headlines and the ways in which the final story is constructed and presented to the public. None of the professionals involved in this process need to be told what makes for an exciting news story. Journalists learn at a very early stage of their career what sells and what doesn't.

This need to find and construct dramatic stories can be considered an additional way in which the media transforms the world of politics into news. Returning to the Politics-Media-Politics (PMP) cycle, one can think of it in terms of three stages. The first stage sets up when something takes place in the political world—for example, five candidates run in an early presidential primary, and two of them do much better than the other three. The second stage takes place when the news media turn the event into a news story by focusing on the most dramatic aspects of the event. In the case of primaries, for example, the media will give a great deal of attention and admiration to the two frontrunners and will relegate the others to a passing mention. The third stage of the PMP cycle takes place when these stories are then distributed to the public, which translates into significant political advantages for the winners and serious disadvantages for the losers. Those branded as losers will find it more difficult to draw large crowds or to raise money for the next primaries. The manner in which the news media makes decisions about winners and losers can often turn into a self-fulfilling prophesy.

The discussion will focus on three areas in which this transformative process is especially significant. The first has to do with the tendency of the news media to be extremely negative and cynical about political leaders, especially during election campaigns. This is an important issue because there is good evidence that the steady flow of cynical news leads many citizens to lose trust in leaders and in the political system. The second is how the news media deal with wars and terrorism. The public has an incredible thirst for news during such events and how the media cover violent conflicts can have profound consequences for how citizens and governments respond. The same can be said about the third issue: the role of the news media in peace processes. A peace process, unfortunately, is often quite boring. It turns out that this leads to an inherent contradiction between what journalists need to produce a good story and what diplomats need to move a peace process forward. Creating the conditions where peace can emerge among enemies is never easy, but the media's emphasis on drama makes it even more difficult.

The Ultimate Cynics

Imagine the following headline: "The President Told the Truth Today." It is, of course, a ridiculous idea (I mean the headline, not that the president would tell the truth). Journalists are the ultimate cynics. If one were to judge from the news we read, it is extremely difficult to find an honest politician. According to this view, our leaders have only one goal: to get elected and stay elected. If this means lying and cheating, so be it. After all isn't this what politics is all about?

Joseph Cappella and Kathleen Jamieson have an interesting theory about cynicism in the news media. They refer to it as: *The Spiral of Cynicism*.[2] The news media, they argue, almost always use a "strategic frame" to cover politics. A strategic frame is one that looks at politics as simply one ongoing contest after another. This perspective implies that everything politicians do and say is designed to remain popular and get elected. Winning is all that matters. Journalists employing this frame often use metaphors that are taken either from the sports world (a "knockout") or from war (one politician is said to "outflank" another). This is a cynical way of looking at politics because it implies that leaders don't really care about the country, only about personal gain.

It is a spiral because the fact that journalists are looking for cynical stories means that politicians believe they need to provide these types of stories, especially about their rivals, in order to get into the news. The public then receives a constant flow of negative news about their leaders and this increases their own cynicism about the political system. Finally, journalists become even more convinced that this is what the audience wants and put an even greater emphasis on cynical coverage. The greatest danger from all this is that people lose faith in the political system. Many scholars believe that this is one of the reasons for the ongoing decline in political trust in Western democracies.[3]

The most telling evidence of this spiral takes place during election campaigns. Journalists are much more interested in covering the race itself than in any ideological or policy differences among the various candidates. There are endless stories about tactics, strategies, intrigues, and polls about who is ahead and by how much. Researchers in political communication call this "horse race coverage" because the only thing that seems to interest journalists is who will win the race.

The most cynical part of election coverage is sometimes called "gotcha journalism." Reporters follow the candidates around waiting for them to do something sufficiently stupid to warrant a headline. President Gerald Ford was caught in a 1976 election debate saying that there was no Soviet domination of Eastern Europe, and he was also famous for falling down (the comedian Chevy Chase made his reputation on *Saturday Night Live* imitating Ford with pratfalls). The political career of Senator Gary Hart ended a mere three weeks after he announced his candidacy for president in April, 1987, when he was caught with a woman on his knees who was definitely not his wife. To be fair, Hart did dare the press to catch him (which proved to be a fairly simple task). Clinton had a similar incident take place during the New Hampshire primaries in 1991 concerning a woman named Gennifer Flowers (this was long before Monica Lewinsky). Unlike Gary Hart, Clinton managed to talk his way out of it and earn the label "the Comeback Kid" (which Hillary Clinton later adopted with much less success in her own run for president). In the British elections in 2010, Prime Minister Gordon Brown forgot his microphone after he had finished having a discussion with a potential voter. After he got into his car, he was heard calling her a "bigoted woman," which became the slur that was heard around the world. It was a huge story in Britain and Brown was forced to go back to her and apologize (he remembered this time to shut off his mike after he left).

This need for journalists to embarrass candidates is a perfect demonstration of the price modern democracies pay for having such an entertainment oriented press. Candidates find it very difficult to run for office without some type of mishap or scandal. Consider some of the biggest stories of the primary race between Democratic candidates Hillary Clinton and Barack Obama in 2008. One typical incident had to do with Obama's pastor who made what were seen as very anti-American comments. This story got a tremendous amount of play in the media despite the fact that it was basically guilt by association. The story then got some "legs" when Barack's detractors claimed that he wasn't sufficiently aggressive in denouncing the pastor. The ever-hungry journalists went on another feeding frenzy when Hillary Clinton claimed to have landed under sniper fire during a visit to Bosnia in 1996. Videos of her visit showed a much more pastoral environment at the time, and Hillary was forced to admit that she had "misspoke."

The Internet has insured that all of these embarrassing stories are not only spread quicker but to a much larger audience. The millions of citizens who didn't catch Obama's poor bowling on the evening news were able to see it on YouTube and similar sites. Following politics in the United States sometimes becomes the equivalent of watching endless episodes of *America's Funniest Home Videos*.

Nostalgia Just Ain't What it Used to Be

The rise of gotcha journalism helps explain another interesting phenomenon. People are constantly complaining that "we don't have great leaders like we used to." President John F. Kennedy is one of the leaders many like to talk about with reverence. Kennedy may indeed have been one of the better presidents, and clearly the fact that he was assassinated had an important impact on his legacy. The fact that Americans watched the entire drama unfold on television also played an important part in this historical process. But there is another reason that Kennedy was so admired: he almost always got good press.[4]

Most historians believe that Kennedy was as much a womanizer as Bill Clinton, including an alleged affair with the actress Marilyn Monroe. A story about the president of the United States having a relationship with a Hollywood star today would be considered the story of the decade. At the time, however, American journalists did not feel that it was proper to report on their leaders' extramarital affairs, and Kennedy remained pretty much scandal free.

Political leaders were treated with much more respect by the press in those days and this policy extended to everything they did. Here too the way journalists cover election campaigns is telling. Thomas Patterson found that in the 1960 Kennedy-Nixon campaign only 25 percent of all the election coverage was negative.[5] By the 1980s the proportion had gone to over 50 percent, and in the 2000 campaign the percentage of negative news had risen to 60 percent.

This discussion brings us back to the Spiral of Cynicism. During election campaigns, candidates have tremendous incentives to "go negative." The use of attack ads has two major advantages. First, given the generally cynical view that most people have of politicians, leaders know that they are going to find it difficult to convince the public of their virtues. Most politicians will find it easier to convince voters that whatever their faults the other candidate is worse.

The second reason is that you get much more bang for your buck from negative ads than from positive ones. A political ad that says how great you are is hardly considered breaking news. But a powerful attack on your opponent ("he's been stealing your money for years") has the potential of becoming a big news story. If the news media and the Internet pick up your attack and make a big deal out of it, it can be a goldmine. Not only do you have a much larger audience for your attack, but when it is being presented as news rather than as an ad the story is considered more credible. Sometimes politicians will pay a certain price for going negative, but most leaders usually decide that it's worth the risk (especially if they are behind in the polls).

John Geer has some good evidence on this point.[6] First he shows that there has been a dramatic increase in the percentage of negative ads in presidential campaigns. The proportion of negative ads rose from 20 percent in the 1970s, to 40 percent in the 1990s, to a record high of 60 percent in the 2008 election campaign. Geer argues that the direct influence of ads is far less important than the news coverage they generate. The news media are certainly paying much more attention to ads, especially negative ads. Geer found that the number of news stories about ads in the *New York Times* and the *Washington Post* rose from fewer than 50 in 1960 to a high of 250 in 2004 with only a slight drop during the 2008 election. The author reports that since 2000 over *80 percent* of these news stories dealt with negative ads.

Perhaps the three most successful attack ads in history were the "Daisy Spot" used in the election campaign of 1964, the "Willie Horton" ad used against Governor Michael Dukakis in 1988, and the "Swift Boat" ad that attacked Senator John Kerry in 2004. The Daisy ad was used by President Johnson against Republican candidate Barry Goldwater. It is important to remember that in 1964 many people believed that a nuclear war with the Soviet Union was a real possibility. The ad consisted of a little girl in a meadow picking petals of a daisy and counting from 1 to 10 (while making some mistakes). At one point a very deep male voice starts counting *down* (7, 6, 5 ...), which sounded exactly like a countdown to a missile being launched. At that point the little girl looks toward the sky, and when the countdown reaches zero there is a flash of light and a mushroom cloud. Lyndon Johnson's voice comes on and says (among other things): "we must love each other or we must die."

The very clear implication is that if Barry Goldwater was elected president, it would lead to nuclear war. The conventional wisdom is that this ad was a factor in the Johnson's landslide victory.[7] There are two fascinating facts about this commercial that are worth mentioning. The first is that the ad was so controversial it was only shown once. If the message was as effective as many people think, it was probably passed on due to *news coverage* of the ad rather than the ad itself. The second fact is that Goldwater's name is never even mentioned in the spot. It is possible that having the voters make to the connection to Goldwater may have made it every more successful.

Another famous attack ad was the Willie Horton advertisement. Horton was a convicted murderer who was serving a life sentence in Massachusetts. Michael Dukakis was governor of Massachusetts, which at the time had a weekend furlough program for convicts that also allowed murderers to get out for vacations. Horton did not return after his furlough and went on to rape a woman and stab her fiancée. While Dukakis did not initiate the furlough program, he did support it as a rehabilitation measure, arguing that it worked in 99 percent of the cases. After Dukakis won the Democratic nomination, there was a constant flow of attack ads about the furlough policy, and it quickly became a major campaign issue. Many commentators believed that this change in the election agenda was an important factor in Bush's ultimate victory over Dukakis.[8]

Then there were the attack ads against 2004 Democratic candidate John Kerry produced by the Swift Boat Veterans for Truth (SBVT).[9] At the time John Kerry was considered a war hero because of the medals he won as a Swift Boat commander during the Vietnam War. This fact was considered a major advantage in his run against George W. Bush, especially given Bush's lack of combat experience. After Kerry had finished his military service however, he became an extremely vocal opponent against the Vietnam War and this angered many veterans. SBVT produced a large number of ads against Kerry attacking him for his criticism of the war and claiming that the candidate didn't deserve his medals.

The Swift Boat ads generated an enormous volume of news. In the study mentioned earlier, Geer found a remarkably high 344 stories about the ad in the *New York Times* and the *Washington Post* during a three month period.[10] Just to give an idea of how successful this ad was in generating attention, Geer compared the amount of news it received to the amount received in six other famous attack ads (including the Daisy spot and the Willie Horton ad). The Swift Boat campaign generated more stories than all of those other ads combined. In fact when Geer looked at the more general news media, he found what many would consider a shocking result: there were 40 percent more references to this story in election coverage than to the Iraq War.

The author found a similar result when he looked at how much the news media covered the most important McCain attack ad in the 2008 campaign. Known as the "celebrity ad," it compared Obama to Paris Hilton and Britney Spears. The idea was that people should decide their vote on the basis of experience not charisma. In this case there were *50 percent* more stories about this ad in election coverage than about the Iraq war. These findings from two different election campaigns provide a graphic demonstration how much election news focuses more on style than substance.

Not All News Media are Created Equal

When one talks about the ways in which the need to entertain influences the news, it is important to again keep in mind that not all media are equally sensationalist. This is important because there is a direct relationship between sensationalism and cynical coverage. When journalists more interested in finding shocking materials than in informing the public, they are more likely to turn politicians into either evil villains or bumbling idiots. When the political process is transformed into melodrama, journalists often turn themselves into the real heroes of the story. Tabloid newspapers cover politics but they are mostly interested in scandals (especially sex scandals), crime, and celebrities. They are much less interested in policies, institutions, and foreign affairs.

In order to understand how the level of sensationalism can vary, you should think about differences among shows (e.g., NPR's *All Things Considered* compared to the *Howard Stern Show*), across different countries (British news compared to American news), and different historical periods (the 1950s as compared to today). In each case, one finds huge differences in how much the news media place a premium on entertainment.

Ellen Hume argues that there was a major shift in the United States towards more emphasis on drama in the 1980s and 1990s due to the rise of a "talk show culture."[11] Talk shows on television and radio became an important source of political information for a large segment of the population. These shows are extremely inexpensive to produce, and the way they compete is to provide higher levels of drama and conflict. While many of these programs are mass produced freak shows ("People dating their mother-in-law: Short-term fad, or a long-term problem?"), quite a few deal with political issues on a regular basis.

The ways some of these talk shows are produced is a great example of the Spiral of Cynicism. To compete for audience share, the producer must find exciting guests. Exciting means some type of conflict, and politicians who don't provide it are unlikely to be asked back (especially low-status politicians). The need to weed out boring political leaders means that potential guests are often questioned before they are chosen to insure they will bring their best "game." The politicians, who are competing with each other, have little choice but to play by the talk-show rules if they want to get more air time than their opponents. The public is then exposed to a constant parade of politicians and journalists attacking one another and cynicism becomes the norm rather than the exception.

Then there are the ideological programs where fiery rhetoric provides a major draw. Two well know examples are Glen Beck's program on Fox and Keith Olberman's show on MSNBC. At the time of this writing, conservative host Rush Limbaugh's radio program was the most popular in the United States with over 13 million listeners.[12] He attracts his multitude of listeners with his spirited and highly entertaining attacks on anybody and anything considered liberal. Limbaugh also makes no bones about wanting to have a major impact on the political process. In what became known as "Operation Chaos," he asked GOP voters in the 2008 Indiana primary to vote for Hillary Clinton in order to insure that the damaging race between her and Obama would continue.[13] Although it is impossible to know how successful he was, Senator Clinton won Indiana by an extremely narrow margin.

One way to think about the differences among news media with regard to sensationalism is to consider the difference between "hard news" and "soft news."[14] As always it is better to think of this as a continuum rather than a dichotomy. At the hard news end of the continuum, you would find less sensationalism and the news stories would be serious and relatively non-emotional. Stories would also be chosen based more on their overall significance than on the level of drama they provide. Although hard news certainly deals with scandals and the like, their more somber tone will often translate into a certain respect for those in power.

The range within soft news programs is larger. This can include everything from investigative magazines such as *60 Minutes* to fake news shows such as Comedy Central's *The Daily Show*. While the former show is certainly more serious than the latter, they share an extremely cynical attitude for those in power. There have been studies of *The Daily Show* viewers, and it is not surprising that those who watch it are more likely to think negatively about political leaders (although it is not clear whether political cynicism leads to watching the show or watching the show leads to cynicism).[15]

Thinking about political humor is important because an increasingly high number of young people apparently depend on comedy shows for their political information. A 2004 Pew Research Center report found that 21 percent of young people (ages 18–29) claimed that they regularly get political information from comedy TV shows.[16] In contrast, 16 percent get information from talk radio, 18 percent from morning shows on television, and 9 percent from news magazines.

If we want to talk about cynicism in the media, we can hardly leave out the late night talk shows where mocking political leaders is a central part of the evening's entertainment. This means moving away from the world of news, but it makes little sense to ignore such an important source of political information and cynicism. Late night talk show hosts frequently begin their show by mocking politicians. When George W. Bush was president, David Letterman had a frequent segment entitled "Great Moments in Presidential Speeches." He would show two short sound bites from memorable speeches from past presidents (e.g., Kennedy: "Ask not what your country can do for you, ask what you can do for your country") and then George Bush saying something inane (e.g., "I know the human being and the fish can coexist peacefully"). The fact that comedians make fun of the president every night is a sign of healthy democracy. Nevertheless, when the president is continually being portrayed as an idiot on so many different shows, it has to have an effect on what people think of the president, and more importantly the presidency.

Here too the power of the humor is amplified by the fact that the best ones can be quoted in the news or appear on sites such as YouTube where they are seen by millions. Not surprisingly, some of the funniest bits in the 2008 election campaign came from *Saturday Night Live*, which has a long history of mocking political candidates. Actress Tina Fey was both exquisite and merciless in her imitations of Republican Vice President nominee Governor Sarah Palin. The clips were not only seen by millions on the Internet but were also shown on countless news and entertainment programs. It is hard to imagine there were many Americans who did not see Fey's portrayal of Palin as a stupid and unqualified candidate. One of the best known bits has Fey as Palin standing next to comedian Amy Poehler who is playing Hillary Clinton. "Clinton" says she believes that "diplomacy should be the corner stone of any foreign policy." "Palin" then adds in a particularly high voice: "And I can see Russia from my house."[17] There can be no doubt that before the dawn of the Internet age, far fewer people would have seen such clips and this would have seriously limited the effects they might have had on the public's level of cynicism.

Talking about the Internet, one has to remember which videos get the most attention. The dynamic is similar to what happens with the news. While a political leader making a good speech may get a few hits, the stories that attract the most attention are the ones which make politicians look bad. This is, of course, just a matter of human nature; we all get a certain pleasure watching the powerful blunder. The Germans call it *schadenfreude*, getting enjoyment from somebody else's misfortune (see the song by the same name in the musical *Avenue Q*). What all of this means is that the increasing importance of the Internet as a source of political information may serve to raise levels of sensationalism and political cynicism to even greater heights.

Media Malaise or a Virtuous Circle?

One of the important offshoots of this line of research has to do with what has been called "media malaise," the idea that continual exposure to the negativity in the media not only leads to cynical citizens, it also encourages people to "check out of politics."[18] When people lose faith in the political system, they have less motivation to get involved. Naturally, if true, such an outcome could be disastrous for democracies.

A good example of this type of research is a 2009 study carried out by Lisa Muller and Bruno Wuest.[19] They looked at the relationship between media coverage and political participation in fifteen Western democracies. They found that the more emphasis there was on corruption in a particular media, the less likely people were to vote. They summarized their findings like this: "By reporting about the actions of political elites in a critical way, the media drive people away from the polls rather than helping them make informed choices and hold the culprits responsible."[20]

Pippa Norris, one of the most important scholars in this field, says that this line of research is off the mark.[21] Norris is willing to accept what she calls the "weaker version" of the media malaise thesis that claims that ongoing negative news can erode support for particular leaders and policies. She found, for example, that news coverage in Western European countries was persistently skeptical of accepting the Euro as common currency and that this had an effect on public support for the policy. However, her study of the United States and Western Europe came to exactly the opposite conclusion when it came to *civic engagement*—people getting involved in politics. Norris put forth a counter-thesis that she calls the *virtuous circle*: attention to the news media *enhances* people's tendency to get involved in politics and this prompts more attention to the news. This point of view is sometime called the mobilization hypothesis. Norris is especially encouraged by the new informational technologies suggesting that the Internet provides an increasingly interactive approach to obtaining political information.

One possibility for dealing with these contradictory findings is to assume that different types of media have different effects on the way different people relate to politics. Think, for example, about the difference between what people are getting from the more and less sensationalist media that were discussed above. Given that the more sensationalist media are more cynical one would expect that a steady flow of negative news could lead people to drop out. Those who get their news from more serious forms of news media would probably be those that are more involved politically.

In a study carried out in Holland, for example, Keeas Aarts and Holli Semetko examined the difference between those more knowledgeable people who tended to watch more public service channels with those less knowledgeable citizens who were more likely to get their news from commercial stations where infotainment is more prevalent.[22] As one might expect, viewing news on the public station was correlated with more political engagement while those who opted for commercial stations exhibited more cynical views of politics and were less likely to participate. This suggests that while certain elites may be mobilized in some type of "virtuous circle," the majority of citizens who depend on more entertaining types of news media fall into the Spiral of Cynicism.

One of the important questions that arise in this type of research has to do with the "direction of causality." The issue is whether people's general orientation towards politics (e.g., cynical) leads them to *choose* a certain type of media (more sensationalist) or rather the fact that they've been watching a certain type of news media is the reason they are more (or less) cynical. This is a valid question, but as long as both schools of thought are talking about a causal cycle it is not essential to have a definitive answer.

Are the New Media Less Cynical?

Will more prevalent use of the new media lower the level of political cynicism among the public? Optimists point to the fact that leaders can now talk more directly to voters and this provides a means to bypass the traditional news media. In addition, the fact that citizens can, at least in theory, interact with political candidates and leaders could lead to more participation. The Obama campaign's ability to get so many people to contribute money and get involved in his campaign through Facebook is a good example of this potential.

There are, however, a number of reasons not to become overly enthralled with what the Internet has to offer in this area. The first is that the most popular Internet news sites look very similar to what one finds in the traditional media. Second, the Internet is above all about choice, and the most popular searches have much more to do with sex and sports than politics. Finally, given the tremendous amount of cynicism that characterizes today's politics, it is hard to imagine any one factor that is going to break the cycle. Any changes that do occur will be extremely slow and gradual.

Although the debate goes on, there is very good evidence that most news media, most citizens, and most politicians will continue to be cynical. This cycle is one of the more significant consequences of journalists' need to keep us constantly entertained. There are, however, other negative influences on how journalists tell stories that are just as important, including the impulse to dramatize war and terrorism which will be discussed next.

The purpose of this section on cynicism was to discuss the problematic effects of having such a steady flow of negative news. It is perfectly understandable why journalists feel the need to tell engaging stories. The problem is that some of the more encouraging stories about the political system are continually eliminated from the lineup. To make matters worse, we depend on the media for almost everything we learn about politics, and it is therefore almost impossible to think positively about either our leaders or about the political process. The fact that journalistic cynicism and the closely linked mudslinging by candidates tends to peak during election campaigns is especially sad.

There may have been a time when journalists were too obsequious to politicians, too willing simply pass on their announcements and actions without any interpretation or skepticism. This too is problematic. If the news media is going to fulfill their role as watch dogs, they need to always ask difficult questions and to keep political leaders accountable for their actions and deeds. Nevertheless, there is an important difference between skepticism and cynicism and it would seem that the normative pendulum has swung too far in the opposite direction. Politics and politicians have both positive and negative sides and it is the responsibility of journalists to tell us about both.

The Drama of War and Terrorism

The media's obsessive need for drama also has a major influence on how they tell stories about violent conflicts. It is not nice to hear, but the news media have a clear economic interest in conflict. *Newsweek* correspondent Evan Thomas put it rather well in an article he published in March of 2008:

> The mainstream media (the "MSM" the bloggers love to rail against) are prejudiced, but not ideologically. The press's real bias is for conflict. Editors, even ones who marched in antiwar demonstrations during the Vietnam era, have a weakness for war, the ultimate conflict.[23]

Nothing gets people to pay attention to the news like war. This was true long before CNN made its name by covering the 1991 Gulf War. The ways in which wars can bring economic benefits became especially clear to the legendary media mogul William Randolph Hearst, who started making his vast fortune in the late 1800s. Hearst produced a series of sensationalist newspapers where truth was often sacrificed in the interest of sales.[24] In fact the term *yellow journalism* comes from a comic strip character, the Yellow Kid, that appeared in one of his newspapers. Hearst, as well as his major competitor Joseph Pulitzer, were blamed by many for helping to ignite the Spanish-American War in 1898. Hearst's newspaper carried extremely graphic stories about Spanish cruelty against Cuban rebels that many believed were designed to put pressure on the United States to intervene. Whatever the truth behind these arguments, one fact remains undisputed: both publishers made a fortune with their sensationalist coverage of the ensuing war.

There are few events that provide more drama than war, especially when one's own country is involved. War's drama is especially suited to television news where viewers can see and hear the horrible things that happen: explosions, hysterical victims and bystanders, fires, neighborhoods destroyed, dead bodies being dragged out of burning buildings, wounded soldiers writhing in pain, and coffins being lowered into the ground. The fact that journalists risk and even lose their lives in order to cover these stories tells you how important they are to the news industry. There are few quicker paths to journalistic greatness than being a successful military correspondent; many of the most important prizes are given to those who cover war.

News about war and terrorism is usually *less* cynical than other forms of political news, especially in the early stages of conflicts. There are a number of reasons for this. First, journalists are also citizens and they too are often swept up in the patriotic wave that accompanies the outbreak of war. In addition, those journalists who may have doubts about a war realize that many in their audience will be angered by any stories that hint at a lack of national loyalty. Finally, there is a big difference between covering routine news about political leaders and covering wars. Editors and reporters have come to believe that political news needs to be cynical in order to be interesting ("good news is no news"). War and terrorism in contrast are always interesting. In fact taking a more detached or cynical view of the violence might even reduce the level of drama associated with war.

War coverage has become even more dramatic in recent years because there are increasing amounts of live coverage and because the military has become more adept at feeding the media a constant flow of visual images and stories. It is fair to say that the turning point was the 1991 Gulf War when journalists were provided with seemingly endless supply of exhilarating images of the Baghdad sky lighting up like fireworks, videos of smart bombs finding and destroying their targets, fighter planes taking off from aircraft carriers, and the explosive surge of cruise missiles as they left the allied ships heading towards the enemy. Many critics talked at the time about the fact that how the Gulf War was being covered more like a video game than a tragic conflict in which thousands of people were being killed.[25]

The initial stages of the 2003 Iraq war were just as intense and also provided a massive amount of drama. The massive aerial attack on Bagdad was cleverly titled "Shock and Awe," and once again viewers were given a "show" that could trump any comparable piece of fiction. The initial narrative of this war was even more interesting because the villain of the story, Saddam Hussein, had gotten away during the previous round of fighting. The fact that everyone "knew" that Saddam Hussein had weapons of mass destruction added another major element of tension and suspense because of concern that the dictator might use gas or biological weapons against American troops.[26]

As discussed, one of the more interesting developments of this particular war was the use of embedded journalists. The deal was pretty straight forward: the reporters got unparalleled access to the fighting and the military got a good deal of control over the storyline. The very fact that reporters spend so much time in the field with the troops inevitably leads to a kinship that influences war coverage. Political scientist Lance Bennett described this relationship:

> Scratch a good journalist and one is likely to find a vicarious adventurer who seeks to be at the scene of the action telling a Big Story. Apparently one could not be closer to the Iraq War story than inside a tank hurtling across the desert toward Baghdad. Nearly every respected journalist (including those too old to go into action, themselves) initially hailed the military embedding

as a ringside ticket to great journalism, a perspective that would bring the uncensored reality of war to the American people. Only later did some journalists admit what they might have seen beforehand: that the Big Story was dictated from Washington, and the scenes from inside the tanks were little more than B-roll filler that authenticated a story told by the government.[27]

Stories about heroism under fire provide excellent war stories. Unfortunately, one of the most important news stories that emerged from the early stages of the Iraq War proved to be more fiction that fact. It was the story of Jessica Lynch who it was said had bravely fought the Iraqi troops before being captured, tortured, and raped by the enemy.[28] She was then rescued from the hospital by U.S. Special Forces who were also able to bring back the bodies of eight other American soldiers. Later it came out that Lynch was in fact unable to fire her weapon because it jammed, and there was no evidence that she was either tortured or raped. To make matters worse, Lynch's friend, Lori Piestwea, was apparently the true hero of the story because she picked up and carried the wounded Lynch in an attempt to save her and later died in the hospital from her wounds. The first, more dramatic version of the events was supplied by a number of official U.S. sources, and the news media were only too happy to pass on the exciting tale. To be fair, it was also the press that eventually uncovered the truth about what happened after Lynch returned to the states.

So what do we learn from all this about the role of the news media in war? First, while it is uncomfortable to admit it, war is very good for the news business. War provides a level of drama that is hard to find anywhere else and this is reflected in both the massive amounts of attention the media dedicate to the story and the tremendous amount of professional status that comes to those who cover these conflicts. Second, due to the level of drama provided by war, and because of the patriotic fever that surrounds the early stages of such conflicts, coverage of these conflicts tends to be less cynical than other types of political news. In fact they can even become an integral part of the government efforts to mobilize the political leadership and the public in support of the war effort.

The enthusiastic press coverage of the early stages of a war has two very real consequences for the political process. First, those political leaders who might have had reservations about the war are understandably reluctant to criticize the government. Given the political climate—which is both reflected and amplified by the news media—such a move might prove to be political suicide. Second, the broad public is often left pretty much unaware of the tremendous risks and costs that come with all wars. It is only much later that the news media begin to tell this other, more tragic part of the story; going to war almost always seems less complicated when it begins than when it ends.

The Horror Show Known as Terrorism

There is only one type of violence that can compete with war for news attention: terrorism. The first major acts of terrorism to attract extensive media attention took place in the 1970s, the most memorable of which was the attack on the Israeli sports delegation at the 1972 Munich Olympics.[29] Those who watched this drama unfold in real time will never forget it, especially because all of the hostages were eventually killed in a rescue attempt. Over the next few decades coverage of terrorism became an important, albeit sporadic source of news.

The "Age of Terrorism" began, of course, on September 11, 2001, when Islamic terrorists flew two jets into the World Trade Center in New York, attacked the Pentagon, and hijacked the plane that crashed in Pennsylvania. Almost 3,000 people were killed. This was a transformative event for both the political environment and the international news media. Terrorism was on everybody's mind thereafter, and should they forget their concerns for even a moment, the political leaders and the news media were constantly reminding them that they had plenty to be scared about.

The ways in which Western journalists and terrorists relate to one another provides fascinating insights about how the emphasis on drama in the news can have an important impact on the political process. It is important to start by reiterating that terrorists are the ultimate "back-door" challengers. Without acts of outrageous violence, few people would have ever heard of the IRA, Al-Qaeda, Hamas, or Hezbollah. Obtaining massive amounts of news coverage is essential for most of these groups because spreading fear among the general population is often far more important than the people they kill. When former British Prime Minister Margret Thatcher ordered a ban on all interviews with the IRA, she argued that publicity was "the oxygen of terrorism."[30]

Western journalists and terrorists have a love-hate relationship. Terrorists hate the Western press but need the media to spread their messages of fear. Terrorist groups have become increasing sophisticated at distributing video tapes to the news media before and after attacks. This publicity tremendously increases the impact of these actions. For their part, and despite their disdain, Western editors can't resist repeatedly showing these clips because they provide far more drama than any reality show. In any case, all of these images are made easily available on the Internet. One of the most grotesque examples of this genre used by some Islamic extremists is the scene in which masked terrorists are standing above their hostages threatening decapitation. These stories are as riveting as they are disgusting. News professionals who broadcast these stories are as repulsed by them as any of us, but given the pressures of competition few can refrain.

This notion brings us back to the idea that the effects of *commercial bias* are far more significant than those emerging from *ideological* bias. When journalists have to choose between their personal political preferences ("I hate terrorists.") and their professional considerations ("Oh my God, did you see what he did? Play that back again."), the drive to create a good story will almost always prevail. Ideological considerations might influence how the story is told but not so much whether it will be told or on how much time and space the topic of terrorism will receive.

Let us go back to the idea of a Politics-Media-Politics process to better understand the ways in which journalists' obsession with drama has an impact on the politics of terrorism. Once again, the cycle begins with what happens in the political arena: Al-Qaeda carried out a horrendous attack on the United Sates that radically transformed the political environment: the war on terrorism became a major focus for the United States and of many governments around the world.

In the second stage, the United States and international news media reacted to this change by setting aside an increasing amount of space and time to the issue of terrorism. Every video tape released by Osama Bin Laden became a major news event and analysts were constantly appearing on television attempting to assess the seriousness of the most recent threats. In addition, journalists began to link every terrorist attack that takes place to Al-Qaeda. Even when no link existed, journalists could argue that that the attack was "inspired" by Al-Qaeda. In the world of infotainment, celebrities translate into ratings, even when those celebrities are terrorists.

The third part of the cycle has to do with the impact of these editorial decisions on the political environment. One positive influence of so much media attention is that many more resources are being devoted to the prevention of terrorism. This added attention can, however, also have negative influences on the political environment. Thus, more frightening news stories lead to higher levels of fear among the population, which helps terrorist groups achieve one of their primary goals. In addition, when terrorist attacks are amplified by the media, it raises the international standing of these groups and makes it easier for them to raise money and recruit new supporters. This standing may also lead to concrete political benefits. There is good reason to believe, for example, that this amplification by the media is one of the reasons why the Hamas movement enjoyed such political success among the Palestinians. The near hysterical reaction of the Israeli media (which is closely monitored by Palestinians living in the territories) provided a graphic demonstration that the group was having a devastating effect on their enemy.[31]

It is important to understand that the decision to make terrorism major news should not be seen as inevitable. It is based on the assumption that the drama associated with terrorist attacks is far greater than the drama that is related to other types of deaths. Just to put this point in perspective it is helpful to compare the number of deaths from terrorism with the number of people killed in traffic accidents. In the period between 2000 and 2008, there were a total of 2,845 Americans killed in terrorism and 99 percent of these people died in the 9/11 attack.[32] In comparison, the number of people killed in traffic accidents during those same years is 334,720, over 117 times the number killed in terrorism.[33] Traffic deaths are seen by most people (including journalists) as inevitable and routine. Terrorist attacks are seen in completely opposite terms: they are considered preventable and unexpected. Nevertheless, given the tremendous loss of life in traffic accidents we have to at least think about the fact that more media attention to traffic accidents could save lives.

There is another important lesson we can learn from all this which will be dealt with in more detail in the next chapter. Most of the more significant effects of the news media on the political process are *unintended consequences* of how the news is created. The vast majority of journalists have no intention of aiding terrorists; they hate them as much as the rest of us. What happens is simply a noxious byproduct of news routines that place a premium on drama.

In sum, news about war and terrorism is inherently dramatic, and this is why journalists have always considered this a wonderful place to find good stories. This coverage of war and terrorism is generally much less cynical probably because such an approach would take something away from the drama. In fact, when it comes to wars, the coverage can even be enthusiastic, which can also be problematic. The routines for covering terrorism are also cause for concern because they can in the end make it that much easier for such extremists to achieve their goals. While the reasons for all this are understandable, they highlight the serious consequences of putting such an emphasis on "good" stories.

News and Peace

The need for drama not only has a problematic influence on how conflicts are covered but also on attempts to end conflict. There is an inherent contradiction between the needs of peace and the needs of news. A successful peace process requires patience, and the news media demand immediacy. Peace is most likely to develop within a calm environment and the media have an obsessive interest in threats and violence. Peace building is a complex process, and the news media deal almost exclusively with simple events. Progress towards peace requires at least a minimal understanding of the needs of the other side, but the news media reinforce ethnocentrism and hostility towards adversaries. All of this often leads to a constant flow of negative news about peace to those involved in a conflict and makes it more difficult to reach any type of compromise.[34]

The role of the news media in attempts to achieve peace can also be understood as another case of unintended consequences. Almost everybody prefers peace over war, including those who work in the news business. Nevertheless, definitions of what is considered news usually lead the media to play a destructive role in peace processes.

There are two major reasons why news and peace make for almost impossible bedfellows. The first has to do with journalists' need for drama: a peace process is mostly boring. We're talking about a bunch of stodgy diplomats gathering in secret meetings dealing with a countless details about how peace is supposed to work. To make matters worse, even if they are making some progress, diplomats are trained to keep it secret because leaks can damage or even destroy the process. Unlike in wars, where journalists are provided with an endless flow of dramatic events, journalists who are assigned to the "peace beat" rarely have anything dramatic to report. Sometimes it's so bad that the reporters end up talking about such burning issues as whether everybody seems to be getting along or what the negotiators had for lunch. For those who are unconvinced that a peace process is boring, I suggest you think about all the memorable novels, television programs, and movies you've read or seen about peace processes. Try to name even one.

Now think about the number of books, programs, and films about terrorism and war. There are simply no profits to be made from peace and that goes for fiction as well as reality.

There is one time when the emphasis on drama is actually good for peace: when the process is over and the leaders decide to have a major ceremony to celebrate. Only then does peace become a major event. The organizers bring out the children, the doves, and the music; the leaders sign the agreements and shake hands (whether there will be hugs and kisses is something that is negotiated in advance). Euphoria is the order of the day, and the news media find such events interesting enough to provide live, jubilant coverage. The minute the ceremonies are over however, journalists head for the hills in a race to find a new conflict to cover.

A second factor that makes news and peace incompatible has to do with the emphasis on *immediacy*. The fresher the news the more interesting and exciting it is. News focuses on events that just happened. While this has always been true— hence the name *news*—due to changing technology people have now come to expect *instant* news. As with many things, however, quicker does not necessarily mean better. Here's an important fact to remember: *news deals with events, not processes*. A peace process can take a very long time, and the news media are not in the business of waiting. This editorial routine makes it very difficult for citizens to acquire a long-term perspective on what is happening.

The problematic inability of the press to deal with processes is true not only about peace processes but also any policy or more general social or political trend. The issue of poverty is a good example. Poverty is a terrible ongoing social problem that plagues all countries including the United States. It often becomes much worse during a recession as more people become unemployed. There are, however, few events linked to poverty that can be considered newsworthy so the topic gets very little attention. There is somewhat more news coverage of unemployment but here, too, these stories are always tied to an event such as a major company going bankrupt or a new government report being issued.

Returning to the issue of how the media cover a peace process, it is helpful to think of peace as a rather long-term investment. Imagine you are living in a war-torn nation and have decided to invest in the peace stock despite the fact that many of your friends are warning against making such a risky venture. Unfortunately, after a year or so you don't really have much of a sense of whether that stock has made any progress. You do get some reports about the talks but, given the nature of news, most of the more dramatic events are negative (such as a breakdown in the talks or people getting killed). By now there are probably even more people telling you to sell. It is not surprising that many people end up pulling their money out of peace and put it into something more solid like defense stocks.

The Oslo Accords

An important example of how the emphasis on drama and immediacy influences news coverage can be found in a study that looked at the role of the news media in the Oslo peace process between Israel and the Palestinians in the early 1990s.[35] The negotiations between the two sides went on for years and, apart from a couple of breakthroughs, there was nothing much to report. There was plenty of negative news to report including a large number of terrorist attacks by the Palestinian groups leaving hundreds of dead Israelis and a massacre of twenty nine Palestinian worshipers by an Israeli settler. There were also many of protests, some of which were violent. In the end, Prime Minister Yitzhak Rabin was assassinated by a Jewish right-wing gunman determined to derail the process. A content analysis of Israeli news found that throughout the process there was far more negative news about the peace process than positive.

The Israeli news media is relatively sensationalist and this was very evident in the way they reported about the violence. After each terrorist attack, all normal broadcasting was halted and only somber music was played on the radio. The news media became the central forum for mourning, and almost nothing was shown that did not reflect, reinforce, and amplify the grief and anger that had spread throughout Israeli society. Graphic and difficult images of the death and destruction were shown in newspapers and on television. Heart wrenching stories were constantly being told of the families who had been destroyed, and television covered many of the funerals. There were also many calls for retaliation against the Palestinians and these threats were also given a good deal of prominence in the media.

The sensationalist tone of the Israeli press also had an important influence on the right wing protest movements who were trying to halt the process. It was very clear from the beginning that the more radical the rhetoric and actions the more likely a group would be heard. Not surprisingly, groups calling the prime minister a traitor or throwing nails and oil on highways were much more newsworthy than people merely giving speeches against the Oslo process. More moderate oppositional groups in Israel felt that despite their large numbers they were being marginalized because of all the media attention being given to the smaller, more radical groups. Interviews carried out with Palestinian sources revealed a very similar frustration. While they were trying to negotiate a peace treaty with Israel, Hamas and other radical groups were getting far more media coverage through the use of terrorism.

One of the important things that apparently takes place during such cycles of violence is that each side becomes convinced that the extremists *represent* the other side; peace seems impossible. This returns us to the principle of representative deviance that was discussed in Chapter 3. Although most members of the public know that the acts of violence are the exception rather than the rule, it is difficult not to conclude that those on the other side are all violent ("all they really care about it killing us"). The vast majority of people on the other side who are not violent are not considered newsworthy.

Some would say that in putting a major emphasis on violence and extremism during the Oslo peace process the news media were merely reflecting a horrible reality. The situation on the ground was indeed difficult, but the news media made it seem even more traumatic. Think of sensationalism as a sort of volume dial. Owners and editors have their hands on the dial and while some prefer to keep it relatively low others prefer blasting the news as if their audience were at a rock concert. Those who choose to raise the volume know that it will raise the level of drama and enlarge their audience.

These differences in volume are not just a matter of personal choice—it is often a question of what is considered acceptable in a particular time and place. Although most citizens are unaware of it, the American press had gone through a number of significant changes in its history, and these changes have had a significant impact on journalists' norms as to what is considered the proper way of covering politics. Michael Delli Carpini, who has done quite a bit of research on the topic of infotainment talks about these changes:

> Looked at from a broader historical perspective, it becomes clear that in the United States at least, we have lived through a number of relatively distinct "media regimes," each with its own economically, politically, culturally and technologically driven assumptions about the role of media, citizens and elites in democratic life. Each of these earlier regimes—the explicitly "partisan press" of the early U.S. republic; the salacious "penny press" of the mid 19th century; the "age of realism" in the latter 19th century; even the "progressive era" of the early 20th century (from which many of the now familiar distinctions between professional journalists and average citizens, objectivity and subjectivity, fact and opinion, and entertainment and news first emerged)—had unique strengths and weaknesses. Each eventually came to be seen as "natural." Each eventually gave way to a new regime.[36]

Israel's press also went through a similar change in professional norms over the years. In the early years of the state (the 1950s), the media was often controlled by political parties and was much more restrained in reporting terrorism and other acts of violence. Among other reasons, it was assumed that overt sensationalism could lower public morale. As the news media became more commercial and competitive, there was an increasing emphasis on drama, and this was reflected in the way journalists related to conflict and violence.[37]

This is not to say that the news media was the primary reason for the failure of the Oslo peace process. Once again, political factors are much more important in determining the fate of these efforts than how they were covered. The process was probably doomed before it began. To mention just one reason, there were too many groups in both societies violently opposed to the agreement; it is far easier to destroy a peace process than to complete it. The Israeli and Palestinian news media took a problematic peace process and made it worse.[38]

The Northern Ireland Exception

There is another side to the effects sensationalism can have on a peace process, seen when the volume knob is set low. We can see how this played out in Northern Ireland. As discussed in Chapter 2, the news media played a more positive role in that peace process due to the positive political environment surrounding the process. The fact that there was such a high level of political consensus in favor of the agreement was echoed by the news media and undoubtedly made it easier to move forward.

However, another factor was important as well—the professional norms of journalists in that particular area of the world. The news media in Northern Ireland are simply much less sensationalist than the news media in many other Western countries, and this had an important influence on coverage of the peace process.[39] The industry is especially conservative, partially because of strong religious influences in that society. This relatively low level of sensationalism has an important calming influence on all of the political actors who feel less pressure to escalate their rhetoric and tactics to get into the news. Many journalists in Northern Ireland have made a conscious decision to lower the level of drama because they realize how much damage a more emotional form of coverage can have on the conflict. One of the most insightful comments about this problem came from a journalist who said that "sensationalism can cost lives."[40]

A good example of this concern is that editors in Northern Ireland think very carefully before sending reporters to cover street violence. They are understandably concerned that the news media, especially those with television cameras, can have a detrimental effect on what is happening on the ground. A correspondent for one of the radio stations talked about the ways in which this sensitivity developed over the years.

> Initially any street violence, any civil disorder at all, we would have had a reporter out on the scene reporting there... As the situation developed further and the media, I'm not speaking just purely about our station but more generally, accepted and realized that people were playing to the camera, they backed off. I mean there have been nights when there's been quite a lot of violence, a high level of violence compared to the start of it, and nobody's gone. It's just been a case of ongoing violence, don't exacerbate the situation by being there, you know, let them sort out whatever they can as best they can, but don't give them the oxygen of publicity to further hurt and insult the opposite side.[41]

This decision to keep the level of sensationalism low has important consequences for the chances for peace in the area. When there is a major emphasis on drama, actors feel constant pressure to be more radical in order to be heard. This pressure is another reason why the influence of the Israeli news media on the peace process was so different than what happened in Northern Ireland. In Israel all of the political actors were competing to get into the news, and one of the best ways to do that was to be more extremist. While in Northern Ireland the media served as a calming agent and increased the chances for peace, the media in Israel were an important catalyst for increasing fears and tensions.

So now you have a much better understanding of the ways in which editorial decisions about *how* to tell news stories can have important consequences for the chances for peace. The greater the sensationalism, the more likely the news media will fan the flames of hostility and violence. When journalists decide, on the other hand, to lower the overall level of emotional content, the news media can play a helpful role in attempts to bring about reconciliation among enemies. The case of the news media in Northern Ireland may be the rare exception that proves the rule, but it tells us a lot about the important role the media can play in conflicts.

Is Infotainment All Bad?

It is worth ending this chapter by providing a cautionary note for all who are so critical of infotainment. If the news were more restrained as some seem to advocate, far fewer people would pay attention. But having more people following current events is something positive. The major reason for making the news entertaining is to increase the size of the audience. This is one of the main reasons why so many people—especially young people—enjoy programs like the *Daily Show with Jon Stewart*. So the emphasis on drama in news also has a major upside: more citizens follow current events.

One could make a similar argument about the problematic nature of television news when compared to serious newspapers. Most people in the United States still list television as their major source for news, although the Internet is close behind.[42] There are many citizens who simply don't have the patience or, in some cases, even the ability to sit and read a serious newspaper. The reason so many people depend on television news is that short visual stories are both more interesting and easier to understand. For many people the choice is not between television, Internet, or newspapers; it is either television or nothing.

Matthew Baum makes the same point in his extensive research on soft news.[43] He argues that this form of news provides many people with an easily accessible and understandable source for political information. He points out that the size of the audience for soft news is very large and that hard news is simply incapable of meeting these people's needs.

There was a rather amusing discussion related to this issue between communication scholar Michael Schudson and political scientist Michael Delli Carpini about which characters from the television program *The Simpsons* represented what the ideal citizen should be and which was a more accurate portrayal of that ideal.[44] Schudson argued that many would consider Lisa Simpson as the ideal citizen because she was conscientious, educated, reasoning, thinking, and probably preferred open and polite political discussions. He pointed out, however, that those who would think of Bart as an anti-citizen would be making a mistake. His irreverence and his obsession with a single issue may characterize those who are highly motivated to participate politically. Delli Carpini picked up on the idea and talked about how many different types of citizens exist in reality.

> ... citizens are made up of a mix of "Lisa's" and "Homer's" and "Marge's" and "Bart's," as well as "Mr. Burn's" and "Mayor Quimby's" and "Apu's." A

world of all Lisa Simpson may be a fantasy, but a world without her would be a tragedy. And, I would add, a world with more citizens like her remains a possibility—if they are given the opportunity.[45]

The thing to keep in mind is that those Lisas who really care about politics have an endless source of books, magazines, and web sites to which they can turn. They have access to hundreds of sophisticated analyses and can also get news reports from every country in the world. But in order to draw in the Marges and the Barts (and maybe even the Homers if it includes doughnuts), we need some forms of media that provide a certain amount of entertainment. The real question, then, might be put like this: Is it better to have more people getting somewhat superficial news or fewer people consuming a more serious version?

As long as news is a business, we have no real choice. The construction of news is an ongoing transaction between those who produce the news and those who consume it. News makers will continue to do whatever they can to expand audience size and this will be even truer as profits become harder to come by in the digital age.

This chapter explained why good storytelling is such an important part of constructing news and some of the significant consequences that are associated with this preference. Journalists know that people are always searching for good stories, and if they can't get it from one news source, the audience will move to another. It was also emphasized that not all news media are alike: some are more driven towards drama and sensationalism than others.

As for the consequences, there is good reason to believe that this emphasis is one of the factors leading to a public who is more cynical about politics and has less trust in their leaders and their institutions. The desire to keep the public engaged also leads to extremely problematic and even dangerous portrayals of the nature of wars and terrorism. Finally, because conflict will always be more interesting than peace, journalists often make peace and reconciliation in the world that much more difficult to obtain. So even if entertaining news has some advantages, it is important to always remember the serious risks it represents to the public's health.

Questions for Thought and Discussion

1. There is a debate in the field of political communication about the problems and benefits associated with infotainment. Most scholars talk about how the emphasis on drama distorts our understanding of the political world. Others say that making the news more interesting ensures that far more people will follow the news. What do you think?

2. It was said that one of the problems with the emphasis on drama was that is it often much easier for leaders to promote war than peace. Can you think of any strategies leaders could adopt to make a peace process more interesting to journalists?

Section III

Media Effects

The previous four chapters have assumed that understanding the dynamics of political communication is important because the media affect how people think and behave politically. In one sense this is the end of a cycle that begins in the political world that provides the initial inputs that are then filtered, interpreted, and packaged by the media and is then consumed by those individuals who follow the news. So the major question is how does the news media's transformation of politics influence the way we see and react to the political world.

It should be obvious that the media do have important effects on all of us. For the vast majority of people, almost all of the information we have about politics comes from the media. Which political leader seems to be saying or doing something especially outrageous? Which countries are going to war and will our country get involved? Have there been any acts of terrorism and how many people have been killed? How is the economy doing? While our friends, families, and co-workers may also talk to us about such topics they too are most likely to have gotten their information from a media outlet of some kind.

Even if it is obvious that the news media have an impact on us, trying to understand how much influence and what type of influence is a complicated business. Nevertheless, researchers in the field have made some significant progress in this area in recent years. We now know something about the types of situations in which the effects are most likely to occur, the types of effects that take place the most often, and which members of the public are the more likely to be influenced. All this is covered in Chapter 5.

5 The Media Get You When You're Not Paying Attention

I want to give you two people to think about. Let's call them Sam and Mary. Assume that they are both about fifty years old and have similar levels of education. It is October 2008 and both are sitting at home watching television and thinking about the presidential election that is one month away. While both stories below are fictional, decide which scenario is most realistic.

Sam is fifty years old and has almost always voted Republican because he feels that the Democrats are too wishy-washy when it comes to the international matters. He also believes that the Democrats are soft on crime. He did vote for Bill Clinton in 1992 because he liked the guy and felt that George H. W. Bush (the first one) was one of the reasons the economy was in such bad shape. He intends to vote for McCain, not because he sees anything particularly wrong with Obama but mostly because he feels that McCain is the better candidate. Sam is sitting in his living room watching American Idol (although he'd never admit it to his friends) when a commercial comes on for Obama. The commercial claims that the only way to lower taxes for the middle class is to raise taxes for the rich. He says to himself: "Hey, I like that. I've been backing the wrong guy. I'm going to vote for Obama."

Mary likes Obama. She voted for Hillary Clinton in the Democratic primary but unlike some of her friends never became particularly angry at Obama about what happened during the primaries ("that's just politics"). She's sitting at home watching the news and a story comes on saying that Obama wants to have negotiations with Iran, and the item includes a slew of people who are arguing that such a move would be a huge mistake. "There they go again," she says to herself, "Trying to find something bad to say about Obama." She decided that the news was just annoying her, so she switched the channel and started watching American Idol.

If you said the second story was more believable, you're right. Most people who follow the news are not persuaded by a single advertisement or news story or even a dozen. The majority of voters develop their political loyalties long before the election campaign even starts. So why do the candidates put so much effort to get into the news and spend millions of dollars on ads if the media do not have an effect?

The news media *do* have an influence on the way people think about politics and not only during elections. But just how and when they have an influence is more complicated than many think. Researchers in the fields of communication, political science, and social psychology have been trying to get a handle on this question for decades. In fact, discussions about the effectiveness of persuasive communication go back even further to Aristotle's *Rhetoric* in which he wrote about the different ways a speaker can convince people.[1]

This topic is known in communication research as the question of "effects." You'd think after all this time studying it we would have a definitive answer about how people are affected by the media. But people are complicated, and it turns out that different audiences respond in their own ways to different types of messages coming from diverse channels in varying types of political circumstances. This notion also came up when discussing the relationship between cynical news and people's lack of political trust. It is because of all these differences among people, content, media, and situations that it is impossible to come up with a simple answer about how political news and advertising affects "people." Incidentally, if we did come up with a final answer to this question, many researchers would be out of a job.

Why is it so complicated? Consider the following situation. In the now famous television interview with Charlie Gibson, Vice Presidential candidate Sarah Palin claimed that the fact that "you can actually see Russia from land here in Alaska" provided her with a better understanding of that country's actions.[2] The news media made a huge deal about it, and every comedian in the world made fun of it. The comment itself as well as the *Saturday Night Live* skit was seen on YouTube and other sites by a huge audience. In short, everybody who pays attention to the world (and some who don't) heard about it. Assume for the sake of argument that at least some people had less respect for Palin after hearing that story, and for some it meant they were less likely to vote for the McCain-Palin ticket. Can such a change be attributed to the media?

The first problem we have is how to separate the influence of the act itself (Palin saying something foolish) from the coverage of what happened (the feeding frenzy the ensued). Even if a survey showed that people lost respect for Palin, we still don't know what really *caused* the change: the foolish remark, the coverage of the remark, or both. The one thing that might help would be a study in which we compared the opinions of those who watched and read about the segment and compared them with those who barely noticed it. But even then how would we know that those who already had a predisposition to dislike Palin were the ones who were more likely to watch and remember the story? You begin to see why the issue of media effects is so complicated.

So what do we do know about the effects of the media on political thinking and behavior? Three types of effects that are prominent in the field of communication: framing, agenda setting, and priming. *Framing* is by now a familiar term that refers to an interpretive theme used by political activists to promote their case and by journalists to tell a coherent story. But here we are interested in finding out how much citizens adopt the interpretive frames that are being suggested by the media. *Agenda setting* has to do with the ability of the media to set people's political priorities. In other words, it has to do with the ability of the media to influence which topics people will think about in a given time and place. The third effect, *priming*, is one of the most interesting effects researchers have discovered. It goes one step further than agenda setting by saying that because the media can influence what to think about (e.g., the economy), they also have an effect on what types of *considerations* (e.g., economic) we use when thinking about particular political candidates and issues.

There are two other, more general, media effects that will be discussed in this chapter: learning and persuasion. The question of whether people learn from the media gets far less attention in the research than other effects but it is no less important. It is assumed that if people follow the news, they will be better informed, and this should make them better citizens. So the major research questions being asked in this field is how much do people actually learn from the news and which kinds of people are most likely to learn. Questions about learning are not, however, restricted to questions about news. People can also learn from other types of political communication such as political advertisements.

There is also quite a bit of research on how easily people can be persuaded by media content. There are many people who have spent their entire lives searching for an answer to this question, especially people involved in advertising. It turns out, however, that convincing people about political issues is far more difficult than convincing them to buy commercial products. Despite this, attempts at political persuasion are sometimes effective especially on certain types of citizens.

The theme that connects all of these effects is stated in our fifth principle: *The most important effects of the news media on citizens tend to be unintentional and unnoticed.* The fact that media effects are unintentional refers to the fact that in most cases journalists are not consciously attempting to influence the way people think about politics. As emphasized throughout this book, their primary goal is to produce interesting and culturally acceptable stories that draw in an audience. The fact that these stories can then have an impact on their audience is best seen as an unintentional byproduct. The idea that the most important effects are unnoticed suggests that when people are aware that someone is trying to persuade them they are less likely to be persuaded. But in many cases, they can be influenced by the media without realizing it. This is one of the things that makes this field so fascinating.

Framing—Here's a Good Way to Think about This

Recall the discussion about framing in Chapter 3. Every news medium uses frames as organizing devices to create a coherent story. One of the examples I used was that during newsworthy demonstrations, the police often promote a "Law and Order" frame while protesters promote one of Injustice. It was also said that the news media are more likely to adopt a Law and Order frame not because they inherently love the police, but because action is always more newsworthy than ideologies.

But to what degree will people who watch such news items adopt a Law and Order frame. Or will they use a different frame for making sense of what they are seeing? Some will certainly reject the Law and Order frame, especially those who identify with the protesters. Others will use their own individual frame. I would bet that some might even use what could be called the "Fashion frame" ("I can't believe what those kids are wearing"). In addition, many will simply forget the story within minutes (those using the Fashion frame will be especially likely to fall into this group).

Let's start with some fairly well known experiments suggesting that the way issues are framed influence the way people make decisions. In a classic experiment that was carried out by Amos Tversky and Daniel Kahneman people were asked to decide between two policies.[3] Here are the two possibilities the subjects were presented with:

> Imagine that the U.S. is preparing for the outbreak of an unusual Asian disease, which is expected to kill 600 people. Two alternative programs to combat the disease have been proposed. Assume that the exact scientific estimates of the consequences of the programs are as follows:
> If Program A is adopted, 200 people will be saved.
> If Program B is adopted, there is a ⅓ probability that 600 people will be saved, and a ⅔ probability that no people will be saved.
> Which of the two programs would you favor?
> Program A or Program B?

Now before I continue I'll ask you to make your choice (no peeking please).

Unless you were over-thinking this, there is a 72 percent chance that you chose Program A. I know this because 72 percent of the people who were given this question in the experiment chose that possibility. The truth is that when scientists analyze this type of issue they immediately know that the two programs have the same "expected value" of saving 200 people. But the reason most people choose the first possibility is because they feel better about a definite benefit than a possible loss.

The researchers then made it more interesting by asking people to choose between the same two programs but framed them differently. If Program A is adopted, 400 people will die. If Program B is adopted, there is a ⅓ possibility that nobody will die and a ⅔ probability that 600 people will die. In this case 78 percent of the people chose *Program B*. This is really the same choice as the first example, but this time Program A looks less attractive because instead of *saving* 200 people you are condemning 400 people to *death*. Death is always an extremely powerful framing device.

George Quattrone and Amos Tversky carried out a similar experiment by asking people to choose between one program that would lead to 95 percent employment as opposed to a different one that would bring about 5 percent unemployment.[4] As you might expect, more people preferred the "employment" policy than the second "unemployment" policy even though the expected results of the two policies were exactly the same.

It is clear from these examples that framing does make a difference about how people make choices. The way the choice is presented provides advantages to one possibility and disadvantages to another. This pattern should sound familiar from Chapter 3, which discussed how certain events (say a major oil spill) give some political actors (environmental groups) advantages and other actors (oil companies) disadvantages. The reason is that such events provide convincing "evidence" that one frame makes more sense than the other.

Here's another framing experiment that is closer to the political world. Thomas Nelson, Rosalee Clawson, and Zoe Oxley showed people two different news items about a Ku Klux Klan rally that had taken place in Ohio.[5] In the first news item there was an emphasis on a "Free Speech" frame: the question was whether the KKK should be allowed to speak to their supporters and for others to hear what the organization had to say. The second item employed a "Public Order" frame. It mostly talked about the dangers of violence either by Klan supporters or by counterdemonstrators. Many more people were willing to permit the rally to take place when the issue was framed as a civil rights issue than when it was framed as a question of public order.

The problem with all of these experiments is that people are told about something they never heard about and are only exposed to one frame rather than two or more competing frames. In addition, these experiments ignore the fact that certain groups have more legitimacy than others. Given that the Ku Klux Klan is considered by most Americans to be an extremist group, those promoting their right to free speech will probably be at a serious cultural disadvantage in their attempts to promote any legitimating frame.

What happens in real life is that when people form opinions about issues, they are usually exposed to more than one frame. In fact, when the frames are contested, citizens will often hear about both frames within the same news report. If you think about public debates about abortion, you will realize that this tends to limit the ability of one set of political actors to dominate the way people think about an issue (which is good news for a democracy). In addition, anybody who cares about this issue already has an opinion, and therefore there is little chance that they will simply accept a different frame being offered by the media.

In keeping with the theme of this chapter, framing is more likely to influence people's political thinking when the frames are unnoticed. Shanto Iyengar makes an important distinction in his work between two types of news frames.[6] "Episodic" frames present stories as individual events without putting what happened into a more general perspective. "Thematic" frames, on the other hand, provide some type of broader context and link the event to something more general. Consider two possible news stories about a husband killing his wife. The first story gives the details of the incident: who was involved, how he did it, and what the neighbors heard. This is a story with an episodic frame. The second also gives the details but then talks about the fact that this is the twentieth case this year of an abusive husband killing his wife in a certain city. The reporter in the second example is likely to also ask what, if anything, the authorities are doing to deal with this problem. This would be an example of a thematic frame.

Iyengar stresses that the use of each frame type can have an effect on which people are seen as responsible for a social problem. When the media use an episodic frame, most people will only focus their anger at the husband. In the second story, on the other hand, the use of a thematic frame will generate anger at the police or the local government.

One of most interesting experiments carried out by Iyengar examined news frames of poverty. Iyengar found that poverty was rarely covered in the news, but when it was covered it was more likely to be covered using an episodic frame that only talked about a specific incident. In order to understand how this might affect opinions about poverty, different types of news stories were shown to groups of subjects. Some were shown news stories that used episodic frames that focused on individuals who were suffering because they were poor. One such story was about some families in the upper Midwest who were unable to pay their heating bills. The other participants were shown news stories that used a thematic frame that placed poverty in a more general political context. An example of this type of story was an item entitled "National Poverty" that documented both the increase in poverty and the significant reductions in federal social welfare programs. Iyengar hypothesized that those who watched the episodically framed news stories would be more likely to hold the poor people themselves responsible for their plight, while those who were exposed to the more thematically framed stories would tend to believe that the government and society were at fault. This is exactly what happened in his experiments.

This example clearly demonstrates that some of the most important effects of the news media are unintentional and unnoticed. The effects are unintentional because the reporters who construct the episodic stories about poverty had probably intended to help these victims and instead may have done more harm than good. If viewers come to the conclusion that the poor are responsible for their situation, there is really no reason for the government to do something about it. The effects are also unnoticed because, unless people are told to pay attention, they don't think that they are reacting to the fact that this serious social issue was presented as a personal story.

Resisting Media Frames

There are other reasons why political context is an important element in explaining the effects of news frames. Think back to our fictional character Mary. Mary was an active Obama supporter so she rejected the attempts by a news reporter to put a negative frame on a story about the candidate. As discussed, most people who make the effort to follow the news on a regular basis tend to form political opinions about political issues and thus they are less likely to accept competing frames being offered by press.

There is some evidence that this not only applies to ideological frames (calling a new health plan "creeping socialism") but also to more subtle frames having to do with how to think about an issue. You will remember that in a previous chapter there was a discussion about the overuse by journalists of what is called the "strategic" frame for covering elections. Cappella and Jamieson talked about the "Spiral of Cynicism" in which journalists contributed to the overall distrust of politics by continually putting an emphasis on strategies and the ongoing contest and not enough on political substance.[7]

It was also suggested that while many people may accept this frame and become more cynical others may be more resistant. In an article entitled "A Spiral of Cynicism for Some," Nicholas Valentino, Matthew Beckmann, and Thomas Buhr examined which types of citizens are most likely to be influenced by strategic framing.[8] Subjects were divided into two groups. Both groups were presented with a news story in which the governor of Michigan, while running for election, puts forth a policy for cutting welfare benefits. One group was given what the researchers called an "issue" frame in which a political expert who said that "the governor sees this as an important issue for the voters of Michigan" and that "he has gained national prominence for his get-tough position." In the strategically framed version, the expert said that the governor is doing this to "get votes for himself," and the reporter followed this up with a comment that the governor is a "shrewd politician who knows how to use the welfare issue to get votes for himself." The researchers also added poll results to the strategy news item to further emphasize the "horse-race" perspective.

The authors found significant differences between those people who are partisans (identify with one of the political parties) and non-partisans. Non-partisans and people with less education were more likely to be affected by watching "strategic" news. They were more likely to say they weren't going to bother voting and expressed less trust in government. If these results tell us something about the general public, it means that those who are unaffiliated and are less educated are the ones who are most likely to accept the cynical framing that is so prevalent in elections news. To put it differently, their lack of political knowledge and commitment lowers their resistance to news frames.

There is one type of media framing that seems to work on everyone. It affects leaders and citizens, those who care about politics and those who don't, and people from every educational level. This type of situation emerges when there is only one *dominant, uncontested* frame that is used by all media reports. This is especially likely to occur when framing national enemies. Here too the power of the frame lies in the fact that is invisible: when everybody assumes something is true very few notice when news stories employ the frame.

Consider the "Cold War" frame that was so prevalent in the 1950s. There was broad agreement in the United States among both political parties on the need to stop the communists at all cost. It was hard to find anything in the American news media that even hinted at an alternative view.[9] Virtually every news story about the Soviet Union focused on the extent of the threat and what was being done to stop it. Those few individuals who attempted to suggest another approach were framed as political deviants or even traitors. When an entire society agrees on a certain political frame and the news media are constantly reinforcing it, it would have taken an incredibly independent thinker to even find alternative sources of information about the Soviet Union. One could probably make a similar argument today about news frames of North Korea and Iran.

Please don't come to the conclusion from all this that when one dominating frame is being used it is always wrong. Sometimes it will be accurate, sometimes it will be wrong, and sometimes only part of the frame is wrong. The United States has real enemies and many of them represent serious threats to the country or even the world. Despite this fact, it is the role of a democratic press and the public to constantly question everything political leaders say. Even if the final conclusion ends up being one of agreement with the dominant frame, the questions need to be asked. McCarthyism probably could have ended much earlier if there had been more American journalists willing to challenge the idea that there were communists under every bed. The mainstream news media should also provide at least some room for alternative views long before they become popular. It is the truly free exchange of ideas that provides the best security for all democracies.

This may be much less of a problem today because of the Internet. As further discussed below, involved citizens have much greater and easier access to alternative perspectives. This is also true for reporters who work for the mainstream media; they too are only a few clicks away from a wide variety of critical views some of which no doubt find a way into their thinking. There will always be some frames that dominate media discourse but there is good reason to believe that those who wish to challenge these frames will find it easier to do so.

Agenda Setting

A second important effect of the news media is agenda setting. The idea of agenda setting is pretty straight forward. When the news media put certain topics on the top of their agenda, these issues also then rise to the top of the public's agenda. How do researchers assess the effects of agenda setting? First you look at the major topics that are getting the most attention in the news. Let's assume that in a certain week the news media have made a big deal over say an economic recession, the war in Afghanistan, and suspicions that the secretary of Agriculture is secretly growing marijuana on his farm. If you conduct a survey and ask people "What, in your opinion are the three most important issues facing the United States today," these are the issues that most people will mention. These are the issues people are thinking about. The tagline for this effect is: "The news media may not tell us *what* to think, but they do tell us what to think *about*."[10]

Now, at first this may not seem either surprising or very important. But when you think about what happens afterwards, it becomes significant. The first thing to realize is that by telling us what to think about, the news media are also telling us what *not* to think about. Remember, we have a very limited view of the world. There are two entire continents that are almost never covered in the American news media: Africa and South America. That means that almost nothing that happens in these two large continents ever becomes a political issue in the United States. This includes foreign elections, wars, disease, starvation, and major violations of human rights.

Just to give you a sense of this, Wayne Wanta, Guy Golan, and Cheolham Lee looked at the news coverage of foreign countries on four major networks (ABC, CBS, NBC, and CNN).[11] They looked at coverage of 138 elections that took place around the world in a period of about a year and a half. Only eight elections received coverage on all four networks, ten were covered on more than one network, eighteen were covered on only one network, and 102 were not covered at all. The amount of coverage of the two invisible continents was almost non-existent. Only one election in Latin American was covered by more than one network and *none* of the African elections were covered by more than one station.

It is important to emphasize at this point that if political leaders had any interest in these countries, they would automatically move up on the media agenda and then move up in the public agenda (consistent with the Politics-Media-Politics process). The same can be said about an issue that was discussed earlier: the huge number of people who die in traffic accidents. If political leaders thought this was an important issue, the media would quickly follow. It is therefore a mistake to only start looking at the issue of agenda setting by asking about how the news media influence the public. One must first ask *who is setting the media agenda?* This is often referred to in the literature as *agenda building* and has been one of the major topics covered in this book.[12]

This doesn't mean that the news media are totally blameless when important social problems or regions of the world are ignored. A truly independent news media would make a point of bringing up important issues that are being ignored by the political elite. This brings us back to Bennett's notion of indexing that was discussed in Chapter 1. If the news media only index what the political elite are dealing with at a particular time, it severely limits the contribution journalists are making to society. Unfortunately, while there are exceptions, most of the topics that are on the media agenda are initiated by the political leadership.

Maxwell McCombs and Donald Shaw, who many consider the fathers of agenda setting theory, talk about another factor that can limit the ability of the news media to set the public agenda.[13] They make a distinction between "obtrusive" and "non-obtrusive" issues. An obtrusive issue is one with which people have personal experience. A good example is the price of gas. People don't need the news media to tell them that prices are going up; they can see it every time they go to fill up their tank. People are much less likely, on the other hand, to have personal experience with global warming (even if they tend to blame it whenever it's hot outside). So this issue is only likely to become a priority when it is emphasized in the news media.

An interesting study about this topic was carried out by Dunaway, Branton, and Abrajano concerning the extent to which people rated the problem of illegal immigration as important.[14] They made a distinction between people from border states, who were more likely to be dealing directly with the issue, and those from non-border states, who mostly heard about the issue of illegal immigration through the media. As would be expected, those who lived in the non-border states were much more likely to be influenced by the media than those living in the border states. Those living in the border states were constantly concerned about this problem. This was an obtrusive issue for them. It was a non-obtrusive issue for the others, and this explains why they depended on the media to tell them when it became an important issue.

Agenda setting effects can also be important during election campaigns, especially primaries.[15] The news media help decide which candidates are electable and which aren't and this means that certain candidates are either on or off the public agenda. Remember the earlier example of the twelve parties that backed candidates in the 2008 presidential campaign (I'll bet you still can't name more than five of them)? The reason this becomes especially important during primaries is that, as discussed, the choices made by the news media can have a profound impact on the ability of candidates to raise money and mobilize volunteers. If a politician is no longer considered a "serious" candidate by the news media, he or she will get less attention and have a lower chance of being elected.

The news media do not just decide which candidate they prefer, they base their level of coverage on what is happening in the political world. At the start of the 2008 primaries, for example, most commentators assumed that Hillary Clinton was a lock for the Democratic primary and that Rudolf Giuliani was the front runner for the Republican nomination. John McCain was considered a long shot. When Barack Obama and John McCain started winning primaries the news media responded accordingly. It is also worth remembering that the news media made a big deal over Governor Mike Huckabee (remember him?) winning the Republican primary in Iowa, but his candidacy never really took off. So here, too, you start by asking what is happening in the political world before trying to understand how the news media responds and transforms it. Nevertheless, once the media has decided that someone is no longer a viable candidate, it is the kiss of death for most campaigns.

Agenda setting provides another example of why the most important media effects are unintentional and unnoticed. They are unintentional because when journalists decide what is most newsworthy, they are unlikely to think about how this will influence people's political priorities. These effects are also unnoticed because most members of the audience are naïve and take for granted the idea that if the news media are making a big deal out of something, it must be important. This type of invisible effect becomes even more important when we turn to the most fascinating of media effects: priming.

Priming

Priming takes the basic ideas of agenda setting one step further. When the news media tell us what to think about, they are also indirectly telling us what to think. The reason is that when we think about certain topics rather than others, it changes how we evaluate candidates, leaders, and issues.

Here's how priming works. Assume there has been a major crime wave that has been dominating the news media agenda. It is right before an election, and one candidate has a reputation for being tough on crime and the other is considered soft. When people think about each of the candidates they have been *primed*—or geared up—by the news media to compare the candidates in terms of how well each will deal with crime. This means due to fact that the crime wave is being emphasized in the media the "hard on crime" candidate will have an important advantage. Researchers Shanto Iyengar and Donald Kinder define priming effects as "changes in the standards people use in making political evaluations."[16]

After the 9/11 attack, for example, Americans' major concern was how to protect themselves from terrorism. Any political leader who was considered strong on this issue became more popular while any who was not linked to the issue of terrorism had a problem. The best example of someone whose popularity rose was New York City Mayor Rudolf Giuliani who was thought to be the leading Republican candidate for president in 2008, mostly because of how he had handled the crisis after the destruction of the Twin Towers. During the Republican primaries, the joke was that every Giuliani sentence had three parts: a noun, a verb, and 9/11.[17] Giuliani's problem was that by the time he ran for president, terrorism was much further down on the political and news agenda and the horrible state of the economy and the Iraq War had moved up. Using the new "economic ruler" by which to measure candidates, not only did Giuliani look like a less attractive contender, but because of President Bush—who many blamed for the economic crisis—the entire Republican Party had a problem.

The difference between agenda setting and priming is that agenda setting only relates to the correlation between the media agenda and the public agenda. Priming takes the process further and asks about the *consequences* of the changing public agenda. How does putting an emphasis on a particular issue affect how we evaluate candidates or decide our position concerning certain issues? This is what makes priming a much more interesting and an important effect to consider.

The evidence for priming effects on voters is pretty solid. A good example is a study by James Druckman that looked at the 2000 race for the U.S. Senate in Minnesota.[18] First, he looked at the news media coverage of that campaign and found that there was a disproportionate emphasis on two issues: social security and the integrity of leaders. Druckman then looked at how much people paid attention to news about the campaign and which factors were the most important in deciding how to vote. Those citizens who intensely follow the campaign in the media cited Social Security and leaders' integrity as the most important in determining their vote. They were primed to think about the candidates within the context of those two issues. Voters who weren't so interested in following the campaign used other criteria for deciding for whom to vote.

There is something surprising in this study. It is those who *do* take an interest in politics that are most likely to be primed. It means that those who are not paying much attention to the election news may actually be more independent in the way they think about the campaign. In this case the lower the level of involvement, the fewer the effects.

The effects of priming provide important insight into why the struggle over the campaign agenda is so important. Political scientists often talk about political parties "taking ownership" over certain issues. The Republicans, for example, are often seen as being tougher on crime than the Democrats. If they can convince the news media that crime is an important election issue, then it gives them major advantages over their opponents. This emphasis in coverage may have been one of the ways Republican George H. W. Bush defeated Democrat Michael Dukakis in the 1988 election.[19] As discussed in Chapter 4, the Bush campaign ran a large number of ads saying that as Governor of Massachusetts, Dukakis had supported a furlough program for inmates that allowed violent criminals out on the streets. The ads themselves were less important than the massive amount of attention these attacks received in the news. There was then a significant rise in the number of people saying they intended to vote for Bush.

The importance of the priming effects became even more obvious four years later when Bush was defeated by Clinton with the now famous four word slogan: "It's the Economy Stupid." The sign was put up at Clinton's campaign head-quarters to remind everyone to always talk about the economy because this was Clinton's strongest issue.[20]

The effects of priming are not limited to the way we think about political candidates; they can also influence political attitudes. Research has shown, for example, that African Americans are overrepresented in crime coverage.[21] Researchers Travis Dixon and Cristina Azocar carried out a very interesting experimental study that looked at how this type of coverage could prime Americans to have more negative attitudes towards Blacks.[22] The question they asked was whether heavy users of television news were more likely to develop a "Black Criminal Stereotype." They hypothesized that when such people were exposed to a crime story with an "unidentified" suspect, this would activate the stereotype and this would have an effect on how they thought about race and crime. In other words, they were being primed to link crime with being Black. They found—after controlling for other factors—that heavy news viewers who were exposed to this "race neutral" type of crime story were indeed more likely to express negative attitudes about African Americans. More specifically, heavy users were more likely to say that any lack of success on the part of Blacks was their own fault and viewers were also more likely to support the death penalty (presumably because they assumed that Black criminal's had a *predisposition* for crime).

An interesting study by Patricia Moy, Michael Xenos, and Verena Hess found that priming effects were not limited to what was being reported in the news.[23] One of the newer phenomena in U.S. electoral politics is for the candidates to appear on late night comedy programs such as the *Tonight Show* with Jay Leno or the *Late Show* with David Letterman. The authors were interested in finding out whether the fact that these candidates were emphasizing certain personal traits on these shows would affect the criteria people used to evaluate them. The researchers examined what happened during the 2000 election campaign and compared those who had seen George Bush on David Letterman and those who had not. Those who watched the show were more likely to think of George Bush as a caring individual. More importantly, this trait became a critical criterion in determining their overall opinion of Bush: viewers had been *primed* to think about his caring personality when giving an opinion about him.[24] For non-viewers the caring criteria was far less important. So when thinking about priming, it would be a mistake to limit our focus to the news media. Entertainment shows can be just as important a source for these types of effects.

Do the New Media Change Everything?

There is an interesting discussion going on in the field of political communication concerning how the advent of the new media may have altered everything we know about media effects (just when we thought we were getting somewhere). One of the more intriguing arguments being made is that because of the major changes that have taken place in the way people consume political information, we can no longer talk about the effects of the "mass" media. Citizens, especially younger citizens, have far more choices about where to get their news, and not all of these sources are going to have the same frames or agenda. This discussion is related to the earlier claim that we are moving from an era of broadcasting to the age of narrowcasting.

Steven Chaffee and Miriam Metzger were among the first to talk about this question in an article with the provocative title: "The End of Mass Communication."[25] They argued that as people find themselves with an increasingly diverse number of sources for political information talking about universal frames and agenda makes less sense. When talking about agenda setting, they put it this way: "the key problem for agenda-setting theory will change from what issues the media tell people to think about to what issues people tell the media they want to think about."[26]

Lance Bennett and Shanto Iyengar make a similar point in a more recent piece.[27] One of the important points they make is that a good deal of the audience for television news was made up of "inadvertent" viewers. These were viewers who simply decided to watch the news because it was the only thing on television. Today people have so many different choices of what to watch and when to watch it that the audience for network news is shrinking. The authors point out that between 1968 and 2003 the total audience for network news fell by more than 30 million viewers. One of the most significant changes in this new era is that the audience is becoming increasingly *fragmented* meaning that there are many different audiences absorbing very different types of content. Given this situation, it makes little sense then to talk about a unified agenda or frame. We may be moving, say the authors, towards an age of minimal effects.

It is far too early however to completely abandon the notions of framing, agenda setting and priming. It is worth remembering that many of the issues that are discussed on the Internet and in the blogosphere are first raised in the mass media. This is certainly true when it comes to the largest events such as elections, wars, natural disasters, and economic crises. When topics get hot, they get hot everywhere, and this means that agenda setting and priming are still relevant in the digital age.

If there is one type of effect that is the most likely to be influenced by the advent of the Internet, it is framing. As people are turning to an increasing variety of communication channels they are being exposed to a much wider variety of political frames. For the most part, this development should be considered good news because citizens in a healthy democracy should learn about a variety of viewpoints. The problem is that many people may use their new found freedom to avoid hearing any opposing views. They will only turn to cable news channels, Internet sites and blogs that share their own view of the world. This behavior is referred to as *selective exposure*.

In any case framing, agenda setting, and priming are still three very useful ways of thinking about how media, in all its forms, can affect us. The digital revolution may very well lead us to change the way we think about these effects, but the basic concepts remain important.

Learning and Persuasion

There are two other types of media effects that have received a considerable amount of attention in the field of political communication: learning and persuasion. The idea of learning is pretty straight forward and looks at how much people learn from the media as well as trying to identify the types of citizens who are most likely to learn. The underlying assumption is that the more knowledge citizens have the more likely they are to make informed choices and this makes for a healthier democracy. The second effect researchers look at is persuasion: how much people are influenced to change their political attitudes or behavior as a result of being exposed to content from different types of media. Most of the questions in this area have to do with the effectiveness of political advertising, especially during election campaigns.

There's good news and bad news about political learning from the media. The good news is that people can learn from almost every type of media: hard news, soft news and even political ads. The fact that one can learn from hard news is hardly surprising. While nobody can remember every individual news item they've seen or read, some of that information will inevitably be retained. The fact that people can also learn from soft news is an especially encouraging finding because it suggests that even those who watch these shows looking for entertainment get something meaningful out of the experience.

Matthew Baum and Angela Jamieson have coined a great name for this: "The Oprah Effect" (although once Oprah's show goes off the air, they may have to change the name).[28] The study was carried out in 2000, an election year in which candidates from both parties made appearances on day time talk shows. They found in the study that 28 percent of Americans reported watching at least one day time talk show, so we are talking about a significant proportion of the public. The researchers were interested in whether people who watched these shows were in a better position to vote "consistently," meaning that there was a connection between voters' opinions about various issues and the candidate they support. Baum and Jamieson found that, all other things being equal, people who watched these shows exhibited more consistent voting than those who didn't watch. As the authors point out, this suggests that soft news may be helping certain types of citizens to be more knowledgeable: "Some may need *The New York Times* to determine which candidate they 'ought' to favor; others may do just as well with Oprah."[29] This is another good example, by the way, of an inadvertent media effect because most viewers seek entertainment but end up gaining more political knowledge.

People can also learn inadvertently from watching political advertisements. Political ads have a pretty bad reputation. They are often stereotyped as a base and vulgar form of emotional manipulation with no redeeming social qualities. It turns out, however, that a closer look at political ads reveals that they have quite a bit of significant content. They tell voters something about the candidates, about the issues that are deemed relevant, and at least something about the policies and legislation the candidates hope to enact. In fact, given that so much of the news deals with the horse race between the candidates, one can often find more substantive information in the advertisements than in election news.

Studies have shown that people can learn quite a bit from political advertising.[30] They can learn about which issues seem to be the most important in a particular election and about some of the candidate's positions on certain issues. In addition, they generate interest in the campaign, and this should assumedly lead at least some people to search for more information either through the traditional news media or through the Internet.

The Bad News about Learning from the Media

There is, however, some bad news about learning from the news media. The first piece of bad news is that not everything people "learn" from the news is accurate. One of the more important ideas in communication traditions is called *Cultivation Theory*.[31] Originally developed by George Gerbner and Larry Gross, those that support this theory believe that heavy viewers of television come to believe that what is shown there provides a mirror to reality.[32] Their minds are "cultivated" by watching too much television such that a distorted view of reality can grow. The researchers were especially concerned with findings that suggested that due to the heavy amount of violence on television, those who watch see the world as much more violent than it really is. This finding is very similar to the previously discussed principle of representative deviance whereby people come to mistakenly believe that the deviant behavior shown in the media represents what generally happens. The theory has received plenty of criticism over the years, but many still support the central claims.[33]

One particularly notable piece of research in this tradition was carried out by Daniel Romer, Kathleen Jamieson, and Sean Aday.[34] They were interested in trying to understand why the American public in the nineties continued to believe that violent crime was a widespread national problem despite that fact that this type of crime had dropped dramatically. The researchers hypothesized that one important source of misinformation about this phenomenon was local news. Local news is infamous for the amount of emphasis it puts on violent crime. In keeping with the tenets of theory, they hypothesized that the more people watched local news, the more they would fear crime, and the more likely they would overestimate the risks of becoming a victim. Based on data from three different studies, this is exactly what the researchers found. People who were heavy viewers of local news had a more distorted view of reality when it came to crime than those watched less.

Here too we are talking about a media effect that is both unintended and unnoticed. Journalists who produce local news focus on violent crime not because they want to deceive people; it is simply good for business. In addition, it is extremely unlikely that people who are heavy viewers of local news realize their perceptions are being influenced by what they see. If asked, they no doubt know that local news focuses on the most dramatic things that happened in their city. But because they are not asked, they remain unaware of how these news reports shape their perceptions about crime.

The other piece of bad news about learning from the media has to do with who benefits most. Here the research concerns who gains the most actual knowledge from the news. As in many things in life, the informationally rich get richer and the poor remain poor. People who care about politics are not only the ones most likely to follow the news, they are also the ones most like to understand and remember what they heard. This difference is often associated with a person's social class. Reasons for this difference include the fact that families with more income are usually better educated, have more communication skills for acquiring and remembering information, and often find themselves living in a culture that encourages keeping up with current affairs. This difference between the classes is often referred to as the "knowledge gap."[35]

One question that has emerged is whether the advent of the digital age could make a difference and help eliminate or at least reduce the size of the knowledge gap. Markus Prior has done research on this issue and his conclusions are far from encouraging.[36] He found that, if anything, the creation of cable television and the Internet has *increased* the gaps in political knowledge. He argues that because people have many more choices, those who are interested in entertainment are less likely to be exposed to news. Perhaps even more worrisome was his conclusion that those who turned to cable television and the new media for entertainment were also less likely to vote than those who didn't have access to those communication channels.

There is, then, a significant controversy in the field about the effects of the new media. The more optimistic researchers are saying that the fact that so many people are looking for entertainment is not so bad because they unintentionally learn something about politics along the way. The pessimistic scholars claim that because people find it much easier to get entertainment through the media, the knowledge gap is getting worse. Confused? The jury is still out on this important question, and hopefully we will have firmer conclusions about this topic in the coming years.

Is Anybody Actually Persuaded?

Political leaders and activists spend a great deal of time trying to convince people of lots of things. They try to convince them to vote a certain way, to recycle, to come out to a protest, to oppose the death penalty, to support women's right to choose, or to move to a commune in Nebraska where people only consume food that starts with the letter "g" (you end up eating mostly grapes, granola, and gummy bears). The most important question for all of these groups is how can we convince people to do what we want?

Anyone who could provide a simple answer to that question would be very, very rich. After all, think of the hundreds of millions of dollars companies and political candidates pour into marketing and advertising. Even if there was some type of answer, however, everyone would soon be using the major formula. If both sides in a competition are using the same strategy, they would simply cancel each other and neither side would have any advantage. In addition, if there was such a magical method, it would no doubt be reported in the news media and people would learn how *not* to be persuaded. Therefore, I would like to persuade you to sell this start-up persuasion company as quickly as possible!

The truth is that the earlier discussions about framing and priming were also concerned with persuasion. When political actors attempt to influence how the news media frame certain events or issues, they assume that if they succeed their preferred frames will then be adopted by audiences. Similarly, when candidates struggle over the media agenda during an election campaign, their goal is to convince people to think about specific topics and not others. Although not all campaign managers are familiar with the term *priming*, they know that getting people to think about certain issues will often persuade them to vote a certain way.

Other paths of persuasion are more direct, such as when a candidate, a political party, or a political organization sends out a message either through a speech that is reported in the media (including Internet sites and blogs) or through political advertisements. There are two major questions that are of interest: (1) How easily can people be persuaded by political messages? (2) Which types of citizens are most likely to be persuaded?

John Zaller, a political scientist who has done path-breaking work in the field of public opinion, has some helpful insights for answering these questions. Zaller has theorized that when someone develops or changes their opinion about something, they go through three states, *Receive*, *Accept*, and *Sample*. His theory is known as the *RAS model*.[37]

The first step in anybody being influenced is that they have to be exposed to some type of persuasive message (they receive it). There are quite a few citizens who don't come into contact with political messages. They don't watch it on television, they don't read a newspaper, and they never read a political blog. They may be exposed to political advertisements during an election campaign or when political movements initiate a campaign, but when citizens have no interest, they are unlikely to pay much attention. Some of these people have opinions about political issues and many don't. In either case there is little point in asking whether they are influenced by the political messages—they rarely see them.

People can also avoid receiving messages they disagree with by confining themselves as much as possible to news sources that tell them what they like to hear. This is what was referred to earlier as selective exposure. Consistent with what was said earlier about an increasingly fragmented audience, it becomes easier in the age of cable TV and the Internet to avoid media sources that carry content with which we disagree. According to a Pew Research report published in 2009, there has been an increasing gap in the proportion of Republicans and Democrats who watch either the more conservative Fox News or either MSNBC or CNN.[38] In 2008, 45 percent of the MSNBC viewers were Democrats and only 18 percent of this audience were Republicans. The CNN audience had a similar breakdown: it was composed of 51 percent Democrats and 18 percent Republicans. When it came to Fox news, the numbers were pretty much reversed: 36 percent of Republicans regularly watched Fox and only 21 percent of Democrats were viewers. The findings concerning which political blogs people follow are even more striking. Lawrence, Sides, and Farrell found that 94 percent of political blog readers consume only blogs from one side of the political spectrum. So one way to protect yourself from attitude change is to simply avoid coming in contact with views that annoy you.

The second stage in Zaller's model looks at whether people accept what they heard in the media as true.[39] This again takes us back to Mary who rejected the anti-Obama news story. The reporter was using what might be called a "Weak on Iran" frame by criticizing Obama for offering to open negotiations with the enemy. Mary refused to accept that frame and her anger was directed at the media for being so cynical. As discussed, people who follow the news on a regular basis usually have pretty firm opinions, especially about major issues such as who should be the next president. These people do not passively watch the news, they actively struggle with it. You might know some people who yell at the TV and some who even throw things at it.

So, you might wonder, if people are so good at protecting themselves from changing their opinions why is there any attitude change at all? This brings us to the third part of Zaller's model, *Sample*. Zaller puts forth the rather novel idea that when people form an opinion about something, they base their thinking on considerations they have on the top of their heads at the time they are asked. People take only a *sample* of all possible considerations, and the ones they choose have a direct influence on that opinion. The way people take a sample is certainly not random. The considerations that are easiest to think about are those that are being emphasized in the news media at a particular time and place.

Take, for example, opinions about the death penalty. Assume that there has been a great deal of emphasis in the news media on the rise of violent crime in a particular state. When people are asked about their attitudes towards the death penalty, the consideration of stopping crime will be foremost in their minds. In this situation the proportion of people who favor the death penalty will rise. If, however, there have been major news stories about inmates on death row who have been found innocent because of DNA, evidence the number of people in favor of the death penalty will probably drop.

If you think Zaller's third stage sounds a bit like priming, you're right. In priming we talk about how people change their standards or criteria for evaluating candidates because of a change in the media agenda, and Zaller talks about changing considerations. This notion of changing considerations is also linked to the ongoing struggle over the news agenda during election campaigns. What is on media agenda influences what is on the "top of people's heads" and this in turn influences which considerations they use to evaluate candidates. If candidates are able to have an impact on the news agenda, or if they just get lucky because of a major event raises their issue to the top of the media agenda, more people will vote for them.

Who Is Most Likely to be Influenced?

There are also some people who are more likely to be influenced by the media content than others. While there is a huge amount of research on this issue, the discussion here will focus on the variable that Zaller has emphasized in his work: political awareness.[40] Political awareness refers to the extent to which people are interested and follow politics and is closely related to the level of political knowledge. Although you might think so, it is *not* the least politically aware who are the most persuadable. The reason is that, as discussed, this group doesn't receive much political information so they can't really be influenced. It is also not those with the most political awareness who are more easily persuaded because these citizens have enough knowledge to reject messages with which they disagree. So who's left?

As it turns out, those with the *middle* level of political awareness are the most likely to be influenced by the media. This group has enough previous political knowledge to receive and understand the messages they receive but not enough to provide counter arguments. In other words, they are more likely to accept what they receive from the media. Now, just in case you happen to be in this group, I should reassure you that even this group is not easily persuaded. It is simply that they are the group that is most *likely* to be persuaded by what they see and hear.

The relationship between political awareness and persuadability is what researchers call a *curvilinear* relationship. This means that if we were to make a graph where political awareness was on the horizontal axis (the x axis) and persuadability was put on the vertical axis (the y axis) the line would not be straight but would look like an upside-down U. As political awareness rises, it increases the degree to which someone is persuadable until it reaches a certain high point and when it passes that point increasing awareness leads to *less* persuadability. This somewhat complicated relationship may explain the mixed results of research on this topic.

Gregory Huber and Kevin Arceneaux carried out an excellent study that, among other things, looked directly at the question of which voters were the most likely to be persuaded by political advertisements.[41] This was an extremely sophisticated study that put a great deal of effort into isolating the effects of political advertisements from all the other factors that may change people's minds during an election campaign. The researchers were interested in looking at people who lived in particular media markets where there were quite a bit more political advertising for Al Gore when compared to those who lived in markets where there were many more ads for George W. Bush. In many ways this study was one of the best in answering the question of whether putting more money into advertising is a good investment for candidates.

The results they found suggest that it is money well spent. They found that these advertisements had an extremely large impact on how people planned to vote, especially on the undecided. Equally important they confirmed Zaller's hypothesis about a curvilinear relationship between political awareness and opinion change. It was the group with a middling amount of awareness that was the most likely to be persuaded by political ads.

This finding suggests that, despite the overall theme of this chapter, there are some citizens who can be persuaded even when they are paying attention. People who don't have a firm opinion about an issue and have an intermediate level of political awareness are the ones who are most likely to fall into this category. Nevertheless, two points are worth bearing in mind. First, when people are undecided about an issue it makes more sense to suggest that they are *forming* an opinion rather than *changing* it. Whether this should be considered persuasion might be open to debate. Second, it is important to remember that this group is unlikely to be searching for political information but rather to come by it accidentally (e.g., through advertisements on television). It is reasonable to assume that those who are inadvertently exposed to political content are not paying as much attention as those who search for it.

Just Like Selling Soap?

One often hears the claim that selling a candidate is the same as selling any other product, such as soap. It is true that some of the same professionals are involved in both types of advertising and some of the marketing techniques have quite a bit in common. Nevertheless, there are important differences between the two types of persuasion. It is because of these differences that convincing someone to change their vote or their opinion about an issue is considerably more difficult than convincing them to try a new soap.

The first major difference is that most people are usually more emotionally engaged when they think about politics. People who vote usually take their decision seriously, and the act of voting says something important about them and their worldview, probably more so than what brand of soap they use. This means that when someone tries to convince them about politics—especially if it is seen as advertising—they are more likely to resist.

Another reason the act of voting is different than buying soap is that the people are only asked to make a decision every few years and, even if they change their mind, they will have to wait for quite a bit of time before they can express that change of heart. Voting is in many ways an investment that you hope will bring you some nice returns. But even if it doesn't, you can't pull your money out until the next election. With soap, you can always throw it out, or if money is especially tight you can finish it and buy a different brand the next time. Hence, most people to take their political decisions more seriously than their shopping choices.

A final and very important difference is that when you see advertisements about soap, they will probably be the only messages you will hear about it. Unless you are an extremely savvy consumer with a lot of time on your hands to go research reviews, almost all of the information you have about the product comes from advertising. When it comes to politics, however, there are plenty of alternative and competing sources of information including one that has been the central focus of this book: the news. People are also much more likely to discuss politics both in person and online while intense arguments about soap are pretty rare. This is referred to in the literature as interpersonal communication and it provides another competing source to political advertisements. The fact that people receive political information from so many different sources reduces the likelihood that any one source, such as advertising will persuade them to change their opinions.

If you want to compare persuading a person how to vote a certain way to shopping, then you'd do much better to think about someone buying a car. For most of us, this is a serious decision; it almost always involves a commitment of at least a few years. Also, when we buy a new car we are saying something about ourselves. Is it a fairly average car or a luxurious one? Is it a gas guzzler, a hybrid, or something in between? Is it a sports car, an executive sedan, or a SUV? Think about this for a second. What are the chances that you are going to make your decision about which car to buy based on a few advertisements? Car ads are designed to have you *consider* a particular model when you make your final decision. The truth is that if you like the car you are driving, there is a pretty good chance that you will buy the same model (or vote for the same party) the next time around.

To Sum Up

The point to remember in all this is that just as the news media should not be considered mere conveyor belts for passing on information to the public, so the public should never be seen as passive consumers of news. This was always true, but many people have become even more active in the way they search and relate to political information because of cable television and the Internet. You need to start with the idea that some people choose to follow the news and some don't. Some prefer to get political information from fake news and entertainment programs, and some prefer to spend a lot of their time reading political blogs or discussing things with their friends on Facebook. In addition, citizens come to the news with different levels of political knowledge and understanding, with different views on politics, and with different sets of topics that interest them.

The idea that the most important media effects are unnoticed is an important one. Whether it be framing, agenda setting, priming, or just plain persuasion, we find that researchers should pay the *most* attention when everyone else is paying the *least*. Most people are very aware when political leaders are trying to persuade them or even when the news media are promoting a certain line. But many of the frames and agenda employed by the news media seem natural and appropriate; the audience is almost never thinking about the editorial choices that have been made or how this might influence the way they think about politics.

There is nothing inherently evil about all this. A change in the political environment often *demands* a change in our priorities, and there is often something positive about the news media bringing new issues to our attention. There is nothing wrong with citizens being constantly challenged to reconsider their beliefs about an issue or a political leader. Too much stability within the public can lead to political stagnation.

The goal of this book is to make you more aware of how the media-politics relationship works so you can be a more sophisticated consumer of news. The hope is that the next time you encounter these situations you will give some thought about how the frames and agenda presented by the media are having an influence on your views of the political world.

Questions for Thought and Discussion

1. Do you think the news media have any influence on the way you think about politics? Do you think it has an influence on other people you know? Give some examples to support your position.

2. Think about the major political issues that the news media are dealing with this week. Based on what you learned about agenda setting, would you say that you have been thinking more about these issues or discussing them with people you know? Now think about the media effect know as priming. If the national elections were to be held today, would the fact that one of these issues was high on the media agenda provide important advantages to one of the political parties? Why?

A Postscript

Hopefully, you now have a better understanding of how the media and political worlds come together. The combined world is one in which millions of political actors compete over tens of thousands of different types of media to achieve their political goals. The goals range from getting elected to something more ambitious such as slowing the rate of global warming or bringing peace to an area plagued by war. Almost all of these actors realize that they have little chance of political success unless they first achieve a certain amount of success in promoting their groups and their ideas to the media.

Promoting one's ideas to the media is never as easy as it seems. The amount of space and time available is limited, and editors can only include an extremely small number of political actors every day. Actors can, of course, start their own blogs or alternative news sites where they will have an unlimited amount of room to express themselves. The problem is that the audience for such sites is extremely small. Those lucky enough to get into the more traditional media will face other problems. Once their ideas and actions have been turned into news stories, they rarely resemble the original inputs and sometimes come out completely unrecognizable. Journalists have their own interests when they construct news stories and, while some transformations can help, others can be quite destructive to their cause.

The public has its own agenda. Political scientists sometimes seem to think that everyone is as interested in politics as they are. The truth is that unless something big happens most people are understandably far more interested in their own lives than in what is happening in their government, let alone in the rest of the world. Those who do follow the news on a regular basis have their own set of routines for dealing with it, and most stories are quickly forgotten. Those news stories that do linger in their minds often go through a cognitive transformation that can be just as significant as the one that took place when the original event was turned into news.

It is also important to remember that those attempting to use the media to achieve political goals are not always directing their efforts at the general public. The news media can also be a powerful tool for pressuring politicians, government officials, or even other countries. While convincing members of the public is often helpful, communicating with decision makers is often far more critical for achieving political goals. In the end political actors want to have an impact on policies, and this means having an impact on those in charge. Whether the goals have to do with global warming, municipal tax rates, health care, or getting a traffic light installed at a dangerous intersection, there are a limited amount of people who can do something about such issues. While direct contact is usually a preferable way of dealing with decision makers, the right type of publicity can be a powerful force in promoting one's case to elites.

The field of political communication is concerned with understanding how this whole process works. The five theoretical principles that were developed in this book should provide you with some insights concerning the rules of the game. It makes sense at this point to provide a short review of these five ideas.

The first principle was: *Political power can usually be translated into power over the news media.* This principle is important because it reminds us that the contest over the news media never takes place on a level playing field. Those with political power enter the media through the VIP gate, which provides them with many advantages over those who are forced to come in through the back entrance. The powerful rarely have to wait in line, they are often treated with great respect, and a select few are considered important enough to have a team of reporters waiting to pass on their messages to a large and varied audience. The politically weak, on the other hand, are often forced to pay the dues of disorder to get in and then to add insult to injury find themselves being booed by the crowd.

The second principle is meant as a reminder that even the powerful can have problems with the news media: *When the authorities lose control over the political environment they also lose control over the news.* The key point here is that while leaders often blame the news media for their problems, they would be better served trying to examine their own political failings. It is true that the news media can exaggerate such problems and make them seem even worse than they are. But when leaders are unable to take control over events, find themselves at a loss when trying to take control over the flow of information, or are unable to mobilize a wide level of elite consensus in support of their policies, the news media will turn on them. The challenges that face political leaders in these areas are becoming increasingly difficult in the digital age, but no one ever said that being in charge was easy.

The third principle looks at all this from the journalists' perspective: *There is no such thing as objective journalism (nor can there be).* One of the most important things you should take away from this book is the understanding that every piece of news you see is anchored in a particular place and time. You are not only provided with an extremely small and unrepresentative sample of all the political events that took place in the world, but they are delivered to you within a particular cultural frame. News is very much a social construction. The power of some of the most important types of bias is rooted in the fact that they are, for the most part, invisible. If you are truly interested in following politics, you have an obligation to collect your information from as wide a variety of sources as possible. While previous generations had to work fairly hard to do this, you really don't have any excuses. This doesn't mean that any of the news sites you turn to will be objective or balanced, but you will be exposed to enough different perspectives to build a more nuanced and complex view of the political world.

The fourth principle deals with another form of news bias, one that has been gaining increasing attention among both pundits and researchers: *The media are dedicated more than anything else to telling a good story and this can often have a major impact on the political process.* The major lesson from this chapter was that journalists' ongoing and almost obsessive search for drama has quite a few social costs. In the age of infotainment we have all become cynical about politicians, and a leader who does a good job is far less newsworthy than someone who messes up. There is also an enormous amount of pressure on politicians to drag their opponents through the mud because it is these types of stories that generate the most publicity. Equally problematic, the emphasis on drama turns the news media into excellent instruments for mobilizing people for war but poor tools for bringing about reconciliation or peace.

At the same time, you also need to also keep in mind that keeping the news interesting has one extremely important benefit: more people follow the news. Even those who confine themselves to shock radio, fake news, or political comedy are learning something about politics. Most of us would agree that this is preferable to having these citizens tune out all together. Those who want access to serious political analysis certainly have little problem finding it. In addition, some of these politically involved citizens are also among the greatest fans of political entertainment.

The final principle explained how and when the media has an influence on the way people's political thinking and behavior: *The most important effects of the news media on citizens tend to be unintentional and unnoticed.* The major message here is that instead of thinking about massive manipulation by the media you will do far better trying to examine the unintentional consequences of how journalists construct the news. The second element in this argument is that people are most likely to be influenced by the media when they are not paying too much attention to it. These points are especially relevant when we consider the three types of influences that were emphasized: framing, agenda setting, and priming.

It is important, however, to also keep in mind the tremendous obstacles researchers in this field face in trying to isolate the effects the media have on people from all of the other factors that can influence them politically. To make matters worse, it may very well be that many of the conclusions we've drawn in this field are no longer true because the age of the "mass media" may be coming to an end. If a growing number of people find themselves turning to those online and offline news outlets that tell them what they want to hear, and if far less people find themselves "inadvertently" watching the news, it's a whole new ball game.

Nevertheless, these changes may prove less revolutionary than they look at this particular point in time. Major news events are still covered by every news organ, and the evidence suggests that vast majority of news stories still move from the traditional media to the new media and not the other way around. So for now we can be pretty confident that what you have learned here about the effects of the news media still provide useful starting points for understanding what happens to people.

This is the end of our journey and, hopefully, the beginning of another one. There are thousands of researchers around the world who spend their lives trying to make sense out of media and politics. If this topic interests you (and how could it not), you owe it to yourself to read some more. As you travel through these works you will find some pretty heated disagreements about the role the media play or should play in politics. But there's certainly nothing wrong with that. In fact for many of us this lack of consensus is one of the things that makes this world such a fascinating field of study. Just as you should never rely on one source for your news, so you should never rely on any one expert to tell you how all this works. One of the key things we try to teach in colleges and universities is how to be a critical thinker. You should apply this principle to every form of information and knowledge that you encounter. It is just as important to use a critical eye for understanding research as it is for consuming the news. The more people adopt this approach, the better citizens they will become.

Notes

Introduction

1. The Pew Research Center for the People & the Press, "Two-in-Three Critical of Bush's Relief Efforts," Pew Research Center, http://people-press.org/report/255/ two-in-three-critical-of-bushs-relief-efforts, W. L. Bennett, R. G. Lawrence, and S. Livingston, *When the Press Fails: Political Power and the News Media from Iraq to Katrina* (University of Chicago Press, 2007).

Chapter 1

1. Mark Danner in a commencement address at the University of California at Berkeley, May 10, 2007, offering his own summary of comments made by a top Bush administration official concerning how they deal with the press. Mark Danner, "Words in a Time of War: On Rhetoric, Truth and Power," Mark Danner.com, http://www.markdanner.com/articles/show/136.
2. W. L. Bennett, "Toward a Theory of Press-State Relations in the United-States," *Journal of Communication* 40, no. 2 (1990); W. L. Bennett, R. G. Lawrence, and S. Livingston, "None Dare Call It Torture: Indexing and the Limits of Press Independence in the Abu Ghraib Scandal," *Journal of Communication* 56, no. 3 (2006); S. Livingston and W. L. Bennett, "Gatekeeping, Indexing, and Live-Event News: Is Technology Altering the Construction of News?," *Political Communication* 20, no. 4 (2003).
3. J. Mermin, *Debating War and Peace: Media Coverage of U.S. Intervention in the Post-Vietnam Era* (Princeton University Press, 1999).
4. W. L. Bennett, R. G. Lawrence, and S. Livingston, *When the Press Fails: Political Power and the News Media from Iraq to Katrina* (University of Chicago Press, 2007).
5. Mermin, *Debating War and Peace: Media Coverage of U.S. Intervention in the Post-Vietnam Era*, p. 1.
6. Peter Baker, "White House Scraps Bush's Approach to Missile Shield," *New York Times*, http://www.nytimes.com/2009/09/18/world/europe/18shield.html.
7. Fox News, "Intel Used by Obama Found Iran Long-Range Missile Capacity Would Take 3–5 Years Longer," http://www.foxnews.com/politics/2009/09/18/ intel-used-obama-iran-long-range-missile-capacity-years-longe.
8. Komonews, "Naked Bicyclists Ride in Protest over Environmental Abuse," Komonews.com, http://www.komonews.com/news/archive/4126851.html.

9. INDenverTimes, "Boulder Police Will Be Scrutinizing Naked Bicyclists in Saturday Protest," INDenverTimes http://www.indenvertimes.com/boulder-police-will-be-scrutinizing-naked-bicyclists-in-saturday-protest/.

10. For a description see G. Roberts and H. Klibanoff, *The Race Beat: The Press, the Civil Rights Struggle, and the Awakening of a Nation* (Alfred A. Knopf, 2006).

11. Ibid. (p. 319).

12. G. Wolfsfeld, *Media and Political Conflict: News from the Middle East* (Cambridge University Press, 1997).

13. Mathew Laser, "Ralph Nader: Internet Not So Hot At "Motivating Action"," http://arstechnica.com/web/news/2009/05/ralph-nader-internet-not-so-hot-at-motivating-action.ars.

14. Evgeny Morozov, "From Slacktivism to Activism," *Foreign Policy*, http://neteffect.foreignpolicy.com/posts/2009/09/05/from_slacktivism_to_activism.

15. Ibid.

16. J. Leskovec, L. Backstrom, and J. Kleinberg, "Meme-Tracking and the Dynamics of the News Cycle" (2009).

17. Interview conducted by the author on November 4, 2006.

18. S. Aday and S. Livingston, "Taking the State out of State—Media Relations Theory: How Transnational Advocacy Networks Are Changing the Press—State Dynamic," *Media, War & Conflict* 1, no. 1 (2008).

19. For a excellent survey of all the different ways in which terrorist organizations can use the Internet see: Gabriel Weinmann, *Terror on the Internet: The New Arena, the New Challenges*, Washington, D.C.: The United States Institute of Peace (2006).

20. National Commission on Terrorist Attacks Upon the United States, "Al Qaeda Aims at the American Homeland," U.S. Goverment Printing Office. http://govinfo.library.unt.edu/911/report/911Report_Ch5.pdf.

Chapter 2

1. Mark Mazzetti et al., "Pakistan Aids Insurgency in Afghanistan, Reports Assert," http://www.nytimes.com/2010/07/26/world/asia/26isi.html?_r=1.

2. Justin Elliot, "The Ten Most Important WikiLeaks Revelations," http://ww.salon.com/news/wikileads/?story=/politics/war_room/2010/11/29/wikileads_roundup

3. John F. Harris, *The Survivor: Bill Clinton in the White House* (New York: Random House, 2006).

4. Dana Priest and William M. Arkin, "A Hidden World, Growing Beyond Control," http://projects.washingtonpost.com/top-secret-america/articles/a-hidden-world-growing-beyond-control/.

5. Andrew Malcom, "Barak Obama Wants to Be President of These 57 States," http://latimesblogs.latimes.com/washington/2008/05/barack-obama-wa.html.

6. See especially D. C. Hallin, *The Uncensored War: The Media and Vietnam* (University of California Press, 1989);W. M. Hammond, *Reporting Vietnam: Media and Military at War* (University Press of Kansas, 1998); C. R. Wyatt, *Paper Soldiers* (University of Chicago Press).

7. Hallin, *The Uncensored War: The Media and Vietnam.*

8. D. Halberstram, *The Powers That Be* (New York: Alfred A. Knopf, 1979).

9. W. Cronkite, *A Reporter's Life* (Random House, 1997).

10. K. Borjesson, *Feet to the Fire: The Media after 9/11: Top Journalists Speak Out* (Prometheus Books, 2005), p. 31. For other analyses of role of press in Iraq War see W.

L. Bennett, R. G. Lawrence, and S. Livingston, *When the Press Fails: Political Power and the News Media from Iraq to Katrina* (University Of Chicago Press, 2007), and E. Boehlert, *Lapdogs: How the Press Rolled Over for Bush* (Free Press, 2006).

11. Bennett, Lawrence, and Livingston, *When the Press Fails: Political Power and the News Media from Iraq to Katrina*, p. 170.

12. CNN staff, "Commander in Chief Lands on USS Lincoln," CNN.com, http://www.cnn.com/2003/ALLPOLITICS/05/01/bush.carrier.landing/.

13. See, for example, Patrick Healy, "Clinton Gives War Critics New Answer on '02 Vote," http://www.nytimes.com/2007/02/18/us/politics/18clinton.html.

14. Rick Atkinson, *Crusade: The Untold Story of the Persian Gulf War* (New York: Marinar Books, 1994).

15. Ibid.

16. Gannett Foundation Media Center, *The Media at War: The Press and the Persian Gulf Conflict* (Columbia University Press, 1991).

17. G. Wolfsfeld, *Media and Political Conflict: News from the Middle East* (Cambridge University Press, 1997).

18. Ibid. see also William L. Bennett and David L. Paletz, eds., *Taken by Storm: The Media, Public Opinion, and U.S. Foreign Policy in the Gulf War* (University of Chicago Press, 1994).

19. Peter Goldman, Thomas M. DeFrank, Mark, Miller, Andrew Murr, and Tom Matthews, *Quest for the Presidency 1992* (Texas A & M University Press, 1994).

20. Wolfsfeld, *Media and Political Conflict: News from the Middle East.*

21. Ibid.

22. W. L. Bennett, *News: The Politics of Illusion* (Longman, 2002).

23. S. Livingston and D. A. Van Belle, "The Effects of Satellite Technology on News-gathering from Remote Locations," *Political Communication* 22, no. 1 (2005).

24. R. G. Lawrence, *The Politics of Force: Media and the Construction of Police Brutality* (University of California Press, 2000). See also S. Livingston and W. L. Bennett, "Gatekeeping, Indexing, and Live-Event News: Is Technology Altering the Construction of News?," *Political Communication* 20, no. 4 (2003).

25. W. L. Bennett, R. G. Lawrence, and S. Livingston, "None Dare Call It Torture: Indexing and the Limits of Press Independence in the Abu Ghraib Scandal," *Journal of Communication* 56, no. 3 (2006).

26. Ibid.

27. Hersh Seymour, *Chain of Command: The Road from 9/11 to Abu Ghraib* (Harper-Collins, 2004).

28. Bennett, Lawrence, and Livingston, "None Dare Call It Torture: Indexing and the Limits of Press Independence in the Abu Ghraib Scandal."

29. Livingston and Bennett, "Gatekeeping, Indexing, and Live-Event News: Is Technology Altering the Construction of News?"

30. Ibid., p. 376.

31. The *Washington Times* Staff, "Editorial: Iran's Twitter Revolution" http://www.washingtontimes.com/news/2009/jun/16/irans-twitter-revolution/.

32. Joel Schectman, "Iran's Twitter Revolution? Maybe Not Yet," Bloomberg.com, http://www.businessweek.com/technology/content/jun2009/tc20090617_803990.htm. See also Golnaz Esfandiari, "The Twitter Devolution," *Foreign Policy*, http://www.foreignpolicy.com/articles/2010/06/07/the_twitter_revolution_that_wasnt.

33. M. Zayani, *The Al Jazeera Phenomenon: Critical Perspectives on New Arab Media* (Paradigm, 2005); M. El-Nawawy and A. Iskander, *Al-Jazeera: How the Free Arab*

News Network Scooped the World and Changed the Middle East (Basic Books, 2002); H. Miles, *Al-Jazeera: The inside Story of the Arab News Channel That Is Challenging the West* (Grove Press, 2005); A. E. Jasperson and M. O. El-Kikhia, "CNN and Al-Jazeera's Media Coverage of America's War in Afghanistan," in *Framing Terrorism: The News Media, the Government, and the Public* (2003); M. Lynch, *Voices of the New Arab Public: Iraq, Al-Jazeera, and Middle East Politics Today* (Columbia University Press, 2006).

34. T. J. Johnson and S. Fahmy, "The CNN of the Arab World or a Shill for Terrorists?: How Support for Press Freedom and Political Ideology Predict Credibility of Al-Jazeera among Its Audience," *International Communication Gazette* 70, no. 5 (2008); S. Fahmy and T. J. Johnson, "Show the Truth and Let Al Jazeera Audience Decide: Support for Use of Graphic Imagery among Al Jazeera Viewers," (2005).

35. See J. Ruane and J. Todd, *The Dynamics of Conflict in Northern Ireland: Power, Conflict, and Emancipation* (Cambridge University Press, 1996); J. McGarry and B. O'Leary, *The Northern Ireland Conflict: Consociational Engagements* (Oxford University Press, 2004); J. Darby, *Northern Ireland: The Background to the Conflict* (Syracuse University Press, 1987); M. T. Fay, M. Morrissey, and M. Smyth, *Northern Ireland's Troubles: The Human Costs* (Pluto Press, 1999).

36. Fay, Morrissey, and Smyth, *Northern Ireland's Troubles: The Human Costs.*

37. G. J. Mitchell, *Making Peace* (University of California Press, 2000).

38. G. Wolfsfeld, *Media and the Path to Peace* (Cambridge University Press, 2004).

39. Ibid.

40. Interview conducted by author on April 15, 1999. See Wolfsfeld, *Media and the Path to Peace.*

41. Ibid.

42. Israeli Ministry for Foreign Affairs, "More Israelis Have Been Killed by Palestinian Terrorists since Oslo," Israeli Ministry for Foreign Affairs, www.mfa.gov.il/ MFA/MFAArchive/1990_1999/1998/9/More%20Israelis%20Have%20Been%20 Killed%.

43. E. Sprinzak, *Brother against Brother: Violence and Extremism in Israeli Politics from Altalena to the Rabin Assassination* (Free Press, 1999); Y. Peri, *The Assassination of Yitzhak Rabin* (Stanford University Press, 2000).

44. Wolfsfeld, *Media and the Path to Peace.*

45. Lukacs, *Israel, Jordan, and the Peace Process* (Syracuse University Press, 1999).

46. Wolfsfeld, *Media and the Path to Peace.*

47. Ibid. Interestingly however after the Israel-Jordan peace process was no longer considered a novelty, the Israeli press mostly ignored Jordan unless something negative was happening in that country. See G. Wolfsfeld, E. Y. Alimi, and W. Kailani, "News Media and Peace Building in Asymmetrical Conflicts: The Flow of News between Jordan and Israel," *Political Studies* 56, no. 2 (2008).

48. Wolfsfeld, *Media and the Path to Peace.*

Chapter 3

1. Alexandra Petri, "Refudiate: Sarah Palin›s New Political Language" (2010).

2. Tyndall Report, "Tydnall Report 2009 in Review," http://tyndallreport.com/ yearinreview2009.

3. Pew Project for Excellence in Journalism, "The State of the News Media: An Annual Report on American Journalism (Year Overview)," Pew Research Center

for the People & the Press, http://www.stateofthemedia.org/2010/year_overview.php.

4. See, for example, Robert Novack, "Immigration and Terrorism," Townhall.com, http://townhall.com/columnists/RobertNovak/2006/07/06/immigration_and_terrorism.

5. See, for example, Catholics in Alliance for the Common Good, "Ohio Billboard Quotes Biblical Call to Treat Immigrants with Compassion and Justice," http://www.catholicsinalliance.org/node/18476.

6. National Right to Life, "Abortion: Medical Facts," National Right to Life, http://www.nrlc.org/abortion/index.html.

7. National Organization for Women, "Reproductive Justice Is Every Woman's Right," National Organization of Women, http://www.now.org/issues/abortion/reproductive_justice.html.

8. G. Wolfsfeld, *Media and Political Conflict: News from the Middle East* (Cambridge University Press, 1997).

9. W. A. Gamson, and A. Modigliani. (1989). Media Discourse and Public Opinion on Nuclear Power: A Constructionist Approach," *American Journal of Sociology* 95, no. 1.

10. W. A. Gamson, *Talking Politics* (Cambridge University Press, 1992), p. 152.

11. Kimberly Kagan, *The Surge: A Military History* (Encounter Books, 2008).

12. Ibid.

13. F. R. Baumgartner, S. De Boef, and A. E. Boydstun, *The Decline of the Death Penalty and the Discovery of Innocence* (Cambridge University Press, 2008).

14. Innocence Network, http://www.innocencenetwork.org/.

15. R. A. Entman, "Framing U.S. Coverage of International News: Contrasts in Narratives of the Kal and Iran Air Incidents," *Journal of Communication* 41, no. 4 (1991).

16. The exception for many years was Peter Jennings at ABC who was from Canada.

17. Examples of studies in this area include R. M. Entman, "Blacks in the News: Television, Modern Racism, and Cultural Change," *Communication and law: multidisciplinary approaches to research* (2006); S. Cottle, "Media Research and Ethnic Minorities: Mapping the Field," *Ethnic minorities and the media* (2000); T. A. Van Dijk, "New (S) Racism: A Discourse Analytical Approach," *Ethnic minorities and the media* (2000).

18. David Mills, "Attack of the Giant Negroes!!," Undercover Black Man, http://undercoverblackman.blogspot.com/2007/07/attack-of-giant-negroes.html.

19. Ibid.

20. Pew Project for Excellence in Journalism, "The State of the News Media: An Annual Report on American Journalism (Online)," Pew Research Center for People & the Press http://www.stateofthemedia.org/2010/online_audience.php#whoareonline.

21. C. Paterson, "News Agency Dominance in International News on the Internet," *2005) Converging Media, Diverging Interests: A Political Economy of News in the United States and Canada, Lantham: Lexington Books* (2005).

22. Ibid. p. 5

23. Here are two books that can give you a good deal of background on the origins and essence of the two perspectives: R. Kirk, *The Conservative Mind: From Burke to Eliot* (Regnery Publishing, 2001); P. Krugman, "The Conscience of a Liberal" (W.W. Norton, 2007).

24. S. R. Lichter, S. Rothman, and L. S. Lichter, *The Media Elite: America's New Powerbrokers* (Hastings House, 1990).

25. Fairness and Accuracy in Reporting, "Examining The "Liberal Media" Claim," Fairness and Accuracy in Reporting, http://www.fair.org/index.php?page=2447.

26. Examples include T. E. Patterson and W. Donsbach, "News Decisions: Journalists as Partisan Actors," *Political Communication* 13, no. 4 (1996); and B. Goldberg, "Bias: A CBS Insider Exposes How the Media Distort the News," *Journalism Studies* 4, no. 2 (2003).

27. D. D'Alessio and M. Allen, "Media Bias in Presidential Elections: A Meta-Analysis," *Journal of Communication* 50, no. 4 (2000).

28. T. Groseclose and J. Milyo, "A Measure of Media Bias," *The Quarterly Journal of Economics* 120, no. 4 (2005).

29. Tawnya Adkins Covert and Philo C. Washburn, "Measuring Media Bias: A Content Analysis of Time and Newsweek Coverage of Domestic Social Issues, 1975–2000," *Social Science Quarterly* 88, no. 3 (2007).

30. D. Niven, *Tilt?: The Search for Media Bias* (Praeger, 2002).

31. If you want examples of this, Google "Press (or Media) in the Tank for Obama" or "Press biased towards Obama." You will have enough editorials and blogs to keep you busy for quite some time.

32. A clip of the routine can be seen at: http://politicalhumor.about.com/gi/o.htm?zi=1/XJ&zTi=1&sdn=politicalhumor&cdn=entertainment&tm=6&f=20&tt=9&bt=0&bts=1&zu=http://www.huffingtonpost.com/2008/03/02/snl-clips-hillarys-edi_n_89408.html.

33. Pew Research Center for the People & the Press, "Most Voters Say News Media Wants Obama to Win," http://pewresearch.org/pubs/1003/joe-the-plumber.

34. Pew Research Center for the People & the Press, "Winning the Media Campaign: How the Press Reported the 2008 Presidential General Election," http://www.journalism.org/node/13307.

35. Pew Research Center Project for Excellence in Journalism, "How the Press Reported the 2008 General Election," Pew Reseach Center for the People & the Press, http://www.journalism.org/node/13307.

36. Ibid.

37. For research and analysis of the 2008 campaign see R. Denton, *The 2008 Presidential Campaign: A Communication Perspective* (Rowman & Littlefield, 2009); J. Heilemann, and M. Halperin, *Game Change: Obama and the Clintons, McCain and Palin, and the Race of a Lifetime* (Harper, 2010); D. Balz and H. Johnson, *The Battle for America 2008: The Story of an Extraordinary Election* (Viking, 2010).

38. M. Hertsgaard, *On Bended Knee: The Press and the Reagan Presidency* (Schocken, 1989).

39. For an interesting take on this period see J. R. MacArthur, *Second Front: Censorship and Propaganda in the 1991 Gulf War* (University of California Press, 2004).

40. See L. Finnegan, *No Questions Asked: News Coverage since 9/11* (Praeger, 2006).

Chapter 4

1. Katharine Q. Seelye, "Clinton Bowls over Media," *New York Times,* http://thecaucus.blogs.nytimes.com/2008/04/02/clinton-bowls-over-media/.

2. J. N. Cappella and K. H. Jamieson, *Spiral of Cynicism: The Press and the Public Good* (Oxford University Press, USA, 1997).

3. See for example R. D. Putnam, *Bowling Alone: The Collapse and Revival of American Community* (Simon and Schuster, 2001); P. Moy and D. A. Scheufele (2000). "Media effects on political and social trust." *Journalism and Mass Communication Quarterly* 77. no. 4: 744–759 (2000); S. E. S. Bennett and S. L. Rhine, "'Video Malaise' Revisited: Public Trust in the Media and Government." *The Harvard International Journal of Press/Politics* 4, no. 4: 8 (1999); M. Hetherington, "Declining trust and a shrinking policy agenda: Why the Media Scholars Should Care," in Roderick P. Hart and Daron Shaw (Eds.), *Communication in US elections. New Agendas* (Roman and Littlefield, 2001), 105–121.

4. J. P. Berry, *John F. Kennedy and the Media: The First Television President* (University Press of America, 1987).

5. T. E. Patterson, *The Vanishing Voter* (Vintage Books, 2003).

6. John G. Geer, "Fanning the Flames: The News Media's Role in the Rise of Negativity in Presidential Campaigns," in *Discussion Paper Series* (Joan Shorenstein Center on the Press, Politics, and Public Policy, Harvard University, February, 2010).

7. On the 1964 campaign see T. H. White, *The Making of the President, 1964* (Signet, 1965); J. J. Matthews, "To Defeat a Maverick: The Goldwater Candidacy Revisited, 1963–1964," *Presidential Studies Quarterly* 27, no. 4 (1997); R. Dallek et al., *Flawed Giant: Lyndon Johnson and His Times, 1961–1973* (Oxford University Press, 1998); G. Donaldson, *Liberalism's Last Hurrah: The Presidential Campaign of 1964* (M.E. Sharpe, 2003).

8. Campaign managers got together after the 1988 campaign at Harvard University to discuss what happened. See D. R. Runkel, *Campaign for President: The Managers Look at '88* (Auburn House, 1989).

9. A. L. May, "Swift Boat Vets in 2004: Press Coverage of an Independent Campaign," *First First Amendment Law Review* 4 (2005).

10. Geer, "Fanning the Flames: The News Media's Role in the Rise of Negativity in Presidential Campaigns."

11. E. Hume and V. Reform, "Talk Show Culture," in Donald H. Johnson (Ed.), *Encyclopedia of International Media and Communications,* Vol. 4 (2003), http://www.ellenhume.com/articles/talkshow_printable.htm#overview

12. David Fokenflik, "Building Bipartisanship? Not Limbaugh's Problem," National Public Radio, http://www.npr.org/templates/story/story.php?storyId=7018083.

13. Rush Limbaugh, "Rush the Vote: Operation Chaos Meeting and Exceeding Objectives," http://www.rushlimbaugh.com/home/daily/site_031908/content/01125108.guest.html.

14. On soft news see M. Prior, "News Vs. Entertainment: How Increasing Media Choice Widens Gaps in Political Knowledge and Turnout," *American Journal of Political Science* 49, no. 3 (2005); J. Baumgartner and J. S. Morris, "The Daily Show Effect: Candidate Evaluations, Efficacy, and American Youth," *American Politics Research* 34, no. 3 (2006); M. A. Baum and A. S. Jamison, "The Oprah Effect: How Soft News Helps Inattentive Citizens Vote Consistently," *Journal of Politics* 68, no. 4 (2006); M. A. Baum, "Circling the Wagons: Soft News and Isolationism in American Public Opinion," *International Studies Quarterly* 48, no. 2 (2004a); M. A. Baum, "Sex, Lies, and War: How Soft News Brings Foreign Policy to the Inattentive Public," *American Political Science Review* 96, no. 1 (2004b); M. A. Baum, "Soft News and Political Knowledge: Evidence of Absence or Absence of Evidence?," *Political Communication* 20, no. 2 (2003).

15. See, for example, Baumgartner and Morris, "The Daily Show Effect: Candidate Evaluations, Efficacy, and American Youth."

16. Andrew Kohut, "Cable and Internet Loom Large in Fragmented Political News Universe," http://www.pewinternet.org/Reports/2004/Cable-and-Internet-Loom-Large-in-Fragmented-Political-News-Universe.

17. Celeb TV.com, "Sarah Palin: I Can See Russia from My House, Tina Fey," YouTube, http://www.youtube.com/watch?v=psyo4JDbJJ4.

18. The original term for this phenomenon was *video* malaise. See M. J. Robinson, "Public Affairs Television and the Growth of Political Malaise: The Case of "The Selling of the Pentagon"." *The American Political Science Review* 70, no. 2: 409–432 (1976); S. E. S. Bennett and S. L. Rhine, "'Video Malaise' Revisited: Public Trust in the Media and Government"; M. Hetherington, "Declining Trust and a Shrinking Policy Agenda: Why the Media Scholars Should Care."

19. Lisa Muller and Bruno Wuest, "Media Malaise or Mobilization: How Mass Media Affect Electoral Participation in Established Democracies," in *5th ECPR Conference* (Potsdam, Germany: 2009).

20. Ibid., p. 20.

21. P. Norris, *A Virtuous Circle: Political Communications in Postindustrial Societies* (Cambridge University Press, 2000).

22. K. Aarts and H. A. Semetko, "The Divided Electorate: Media Use and Political Involvement," *The Journal of Politics* 65, no. 3 (2008).

23. Evan Thomas, "The Myth of Objectivity," *Newsweek,* March 1, 2008.

24. M. A. Lee and N. Solomon, *Unreliable Sources: A Guide to Detecting Bias in News Media* (Lyle Stuart, 1991); D. Nasaw, *The Chief: The Life of William Randolph Hearst* (Mariner Books, 2001); B. H. Procter, *William Randolph Hearst: The Early Years, 1863–1910* (Oxford University Press, 1998).

25. On the role of the media in the Gulf War see Rick Atkinson, *Crusade: The Untold Story of the Persian Gulf War* (New York: Marinar Books, 1994); William L. Bennett and David L. Paletz, ed., *Taken by Storm: The Media, Pubic Opinion, and U.S. Foreign Policy in the Gulf War* (University of Chicago Press, 1994); W. Dorman and S. Livingston, "News and Historical Content: The Establishment Phase of the Persian Gulf Policy Debate," in *Taken by Storm: The Media, Pubic Opinion, and U.S. Foreign Policy in the Gulf War;* Gannett Foundation Media Center, *The Media at War: The Press and the Persian Gulf Conflict* (Columbia University, 1991); J. A. Krosnick and L. A. Brannon, "The Impact of the Gulf War on the Ingredients of Presidential Evaluations: Multidimensional Effects of Political Involvement," *American Political Science Review* (1993); J. R. MacArthur, *Second Front: Censorship and Propaganda in the 1991 Gulf War* (University of California Press, 2004); G. Wolfsfeld, *Media and Political Conflict: News from the Middle East* (Cambridge University Press, 1997).

26. On the role of the media in the 2003 Iraq war see S. Kull, C. Ramsay, and E. Lewis, "Misperceptions, the Media, and the Iraq War," *Political Science Quarterly* 118, no. 4 (2003); Sean Aday, Steven Livingston, and Maeve Hebert, "Embedding the Truth: A Cross-Cultural Analysis of Objectivity and Television Coverage of the Iraq War," *The Harvard International Journal of Press/Politics* 10, no. 3 (2005); W. L. Bennett, R. G. Lawrence, and S. Livingston, *When the Press Fails: Political Power and the News Media from Iraq to Katrina* (University of Chicago Press, 2007); H. Tumber and J. Palmer, *Media at War: The Iraq Crisis* (Sage Publications, 2004); J.

Lewis, *Shoot First and Ask Questions Later: Media Coverage of the 2003 Iraq War* (Peter Lang, 2006).

27. W. L. Bennett, "Operation Perfect Storm: The Press and the Iraq War," *Political Communication Report* 13, no. 3 (2003).

28. For different perspectives on this incident see J. Kampfner, "The Truth About Jessica," *The Guardian* 15 (2003); R. Bragg, *I Am a Soldier, Too: The Jessica Lynch Story* (Alfred A. Knopf, 2003); B. Tucker and P. L. Walton, "From General's Daughter to Coal Miner's Daughter: Spinning and Counter-Spinning Jessica Lynch," *Canadian Review of American Studies* 36, no. 3 (2006).

29. A. J. Klein, *Striking Back: The 1972 Munich Olympics Massacre and Israel's Deadly Response* (Random House, 2007); S. Reeve, *One Day in September: The Full Story of the 1972 Munich Olympics Massacre and the Israeli Revenge Operation" Wrath of God"* (Arcade, 2000).

30. This quote appears in dozens of articles. One example is Michael Stohl, "Old Myths, New Fantasies and the Enduring Realities of Terrorism," *Critical Studies in Terrorism* 1, no. 1 (2008).

31. G. Wolfsfeld, *Media and the Path to Peace* (Cambridge University Press, 2004).

32. Reuters, "Timeline: Attacks on U.S. Targets," Reuters, http://www.reuters.com/article/idUSTRE6411QA20100502.

33. National Highway Traffic Safety Administration, "Fatal Crashes 1994-2008," http://www-fars.nhtsa.dot.gov/Trends/TrendsGeneral.aspx.

34. Wolfsfeld, *Media and the Path to Peace.*

35. Ibid.

36. Michael X. Delli Carpini, "The Inherent Arbitrariness of the 'News' Versus 'Enterntainment' Distinction," Social Science Research Council, http://publicsphere.ssrc.org/delli-carpini-the-inherent-arbitrariness-of-the-news-versus-entertainment-distinction/.

37. Wolfsfeld, *Media and the Path to Peace.*

38. Ibid.

39. Ibid.

40. Ibid., p. 178.

41. Interview carried out by author April 13, 1999. See Wolfsfeld, *Media and the Path to Peace.*

42. Pew Internet and American Life Project, "The New News Landscape: Rise of the Internet," http://pewresearch.org/pubs/1508/internet-cell-phone-users-news-social-experience.

43. Max Baum, "A Coalition of the Unrestrained: Mass Media, Electoral Institutions and the Constraining Effect of Public Opinion Regarding Iraq," in *2008 Meeting of the American Political Science Association* (Boston, MA: 2008); Baum, "Circling the Wagons: Soft News and Isolationism in American Public Opinion"; Baum, "Sex, Lies, and War: How Soft News Brings Foreign Policy to the Inattentive Public"; Baum, "Soft News and Political Knowledge: Evidence of Absence or Absence of Evidence?"; Baum and Jamison, "The Oprah Effect: How Soft News Helps Inattentive Citizens Vote Consistently."

44. The Schudson piece can be found at Michael Schudson, "A Family of Public Spheres," Social Science Research Council, http://publicsphere.ssrc.org/schudson-a-family-of-public-spheres/; Delli Carpini, "The Inherent Arbitrariness of the 'News' Versus 'Entertainment' Distinction."

45. Delli Carpini, "The Inherent Arbitrariness of the 'News' Versus 'Entertainment'Distinction."

Chapter 5

1. E. Garver, *Aristotle's Rhetoric: An Art of Character* (University of Chicago Press, 1994).
2. ABC News, "Sarah Palin ABC Gibson Interview — Russia Is Our Neighbor!," YouTube, http://www.youtube.com/watch?v=cdftnFjQfzs.
3. A. Tversky and D. Kahneman, "The Framing of Decisions and the Psychology of Choice," *Science* 211, no. 4481 (1981).
4. George A. Quattrone and Amos Tversky, "Rational and Psychological Analyses of Political Choice," *The American Political Science Review* 82, no. 3 (1988).
5. T. E. Nelson, R. A. Clawson, and Z. M. Oxley, "Media Framing of a Civil Liberties Conflict and Its Effect on Tolerance," *American Political Science Review* 91 (1997).
6. S. Iyengar, *Is Anyone Responsible?: How Television Frames Political Issues* (University of Chicago Press, 1994).
7. J. N. Cappella and K. H. Jamieson, *Spiral of Cynicism: The Press and the Public Good* (Oxford University Press, 1997).
8. N. A. Valentino, M. N. Beckmann, and T. A. Buhr, "A Spiral of Cynicism for Some: The Contingent Effects of Campaign News Frames on Participation and Confidence in Government," *Political Communication* 18, no. 4 (2001).
9. R. M. Entman, *Projections of Power: Framing News, Public Opinion, and US Foreign Policy* (University Of Chicago Press, 2004); D. C. Hallin, *The Uncensored War: The Media and Vietnam* (University of California Press, 1989); W. A. Gamson, *Talking Politics* (Cambridge University Press, 1992).
10. M. E. McCombs and D. L. Shaw, "The Agenda-Setting Function of Mass Media," *Public Opinion Quarterly* 36, no. 2 (1972).
11. W. Wanta, G. Golan, and C. Lee, "Agenda Setting and International News: Media Influence on Public Perceptions of Foreign Nations," *Journalism and Mass Communication Quartlerly* 81, no. 2 (2004).
12. Here are some interesting studies that deal with agenda building: T. Sheafer and I. Gabay, "Mediated Public Diplomacy: A Strategic Contest over International Agenda Building and Frame Building," *Political Communication* 26, no. 4 (2009); T. Sheafer and G. Weimann, "Agenda Building, Agenda Setting, Priming, Individual Voting Intentions, and the Aggregate Results: An Analysis of Four Israeli Elections," *The Journal of Communication* 55, no. 2 (2005); L. Van Noije, J. Kleinnijenhuis, and D. Oegema, "Loss of Parliamentary Control Due to Mediatization and Europeanization: A Longitudinal and Cross-Sectional Analysis of Agenda Building in the United Kingdom and the Netherlands," *British Journal of Political Science* 38, no. 3 (2008); W. Wanta and Y. Kalyango Jr,, "Terrorism and Africa: A Study of Agenda Building in the United States," *International Journal of Public Opinion Research* 19, no. 4 (2007).
13. M. McCombs, "A Look at Agenda-Setting: Past, Present and Future," *Journalism Studies* 6, no. 4 (2005).
14. J. Dunaway, R. P. Branton, and M. A. Abrajano, "Agenda Setting, Public Opinion, and the Issue of Immigration Reform," *Social Science Quarterly* 91, no. 2 (2010).
15. There has been some extremely interesting research on agenda setting and priming in Israeli elections that raises new issues concerning the relationship between these

two processes. See T. Sheafer, "How to Evaluate It: The Role of Story-Evaluative Tone in Agenda Setting and Priming," *Journal of Communication* 57, no. 1 (2007); Sheafer and Weimann, "Agenda Building, Agenda Setting, Priming, Individual Voting Intentions, and the Aggregate Results: An Analysis of Four Israeli Elections"; M. Balmas and T. Sheafer, "Candidate Image in Election Campaigns: Attribute Agenda Setting, Affective Priming, and Voting Intentions," *International Journal of Public Opinion Research* 22, no. 2 (2010).

16. S. Iyengar and D. R. Kinder, *News That Matters: Television and American Opinion* (University of Chicago Press, 1988), p. 63.

17. The attack was first initiated by then Senator Biden. See Joelle Farrell, "A Noun, a Verb and 9/11," Concord Monitor, http://www.concordmonitor.com/article/noun-verb-and-911.

18. J. N. Druckman, "Priming the Vote: Campaign Effects in a U.S. Senate Election," *Political Psychology* (2004).

19. D. R. Runkel, *Campaign for President: The Managers Look at '88* (Auburn House, 1989).

20. Interestingly, while conventional wisdom has it that the economic issue was the critical policy issue to bring about Clinton's victory in 1992, at least one researcher found that the differences between the candidates on abortion was far more important. A. I. Abramowitz, "It's Abortion, Stupid: Policy Voting in the 1992 Presidential Election," *The Journal of Politics* 57, no. 1 (2009).

21. R. M. Entman and A. Rojecki, *The Black Image in the White Mind: Media and Race in America* (University of Chicago Press, 2001).

22. T. L. Dixon and C. L. Azocar, "Priming Crime and Activating Blackness: Understanding the Psychological Impact of the Overrepresentation of Blacks as Lawbreakers on Television News," *Journal of Communication* 57, no. 2 (2007).

23. P. Moy, M. A. Xenos, and V. K. Hess, "Priming Effects of Late-Night Comedy," *International Journal of Public Opinion Research* 18, no. 2 (2006).

24. The researchers did not find, however, a similar priming effect for Al Gore. They suggest one reason for this difference was that people were just *forming* an opinion of Bush in 2000 while they already knew Al Gore because he had served as vice president.

25. S. H. Chaffee and M. J. Metzger, "The End of Mass Communication?", *Mass Communication & Society* 4, no. 4 (2001).

26. Ibid., p. 375.

27. W. L. Bennett and S. Iyengar, "A New Era of Minimal Effects? The Changing Foundations of Political Communication," *Journal of Communication* 58, no. 4 (2008).

28. M. A. Baum and A. S. Jamison, "The Oprah Effect: How Soft News Helps Inattentive Citizens Vote Consistently," *Journal of Politics* 68, no. 4 (2006).

29. Ibid., p. 947.

30. Examples of research in this area include: N. A. Valentino, V. L. Hutchings, and D. Williams, "The Impact of Political Advertising on Knowledge, Internet Information Seeking, and Candidate Preference," *Journal of Communication* 54, no. 2 (2004); K. Goldstein and T. N. Ridout, "Measuring the Effects of Televised Political Advertising in the United States, " *Annual Review of Political Science* 7: 205–26 (2004); L. L. Kaid and M. Postelnicu, "Political Advertising in the 2004 Election: Comparison of Traditional Television and Internet Messages," *American Behavioral Scientist* 49, no. 2 (2005).

31. For a review of research in this area see M. Morgan and J. Shanahan, "Two Decades of Cultivation Analysis: An Appraisal and Meta-Analysis," *Communication Yearbook* 20 (1997).

32. G. Gerbner and L. Gross, "Living with Television: The Violence Profile," *Journal of Communication* 26, no. 2 (1976).

33. To better understand the controversy see Morgan and Shanahan, "Two Decades of Cultivation Analysis: An Appraisal and Meta-Analysis."

34. D. Romer, K. H. Jamieson, and S. Aday, "Television News and the Cultivation of Fear of Crime," *Journal of Communication* 53, no. 1 (2003).

35. For a review of research in this area see K. Viswanath and J. R. Finnegan, "The Knowledge Gap Hypothesis: Twenty-Five Years Later," in In B. Burleson (Ed.), *Communication Yearbook* 19 (Sage, 1996), 187–227.

36. M. Prior, "News Vs. Entertainment: How Increasing Media Choice Widens Gaps in Political Knowledge and Turnout," *American Journal of Political Science* 49, no. 3 (2005).

37. J. Zaller, The Nature and Origins of Mass Opinion (Cambridge University Press, 1992); Zaller, J. (1996). "The Myth of Massive Media Impact Revived: New Support for a Discredited Idea," In Diana Carole Mutz, Paul M. Sniderman, & Richard A. Brody (Eds.), *Political Persuasion and Attitude Change.* Ann Arbor, University of Michigan Press: 17–78.

38. Pew Research Center for the People & the Press, "Partisanship and Cable News Audiences," Pew Research Center Publiciations, http://pewresearch.org/pubs/1395/partisanship-fox-news-and--other-cable-news-audiences.

39. Zaller, *The Nature and Origins of Mass Opinion.*

40. Ibid.

41. G. A. Huber and K. Arceneaux, "Identifying the Persuasive Effects of Presidential Advertising," *American Journal of Political Science* 51, no. 4 (2007). It is also interesting to note that in contrast to other studies Huber and Arceneaux found little learning from political advertising.

References

Aarts, K., and H. A. Semetko. "The Divided Electorate: Media Use and Political Involvement." *The Journal of Politics* 65, no. 3 (2008): 759–84.

ABC News. "Sarah Palin ABC Gibson Interview — Russia Is Our Neighbor!" YouTube, http://www.youtube.com/watch?v=cdftnFjQfzs.

Abramowitz, A. I. "It's Abortion, Stupid: Policy Voting in the 1992 Presidential Election." *The Journal of Politics* 57, no. 1 (2009): 176–86.

Aday, S., and S. Livingston. "Taking the State out of State-Media Relations Theory: How Transnational Advocacy Networks Are Changing the Press-State Dynamic." *Media, War & Conflict* 1, no. 1 (2008): 99–107.

Aday, S., S. Livingston, and M. Hebert. "Embedding the Truth: A Cross-Cultural Analysis of Objectivity and Television Coverage of the Iraq War." *The Harvard International Journal of Press/Politics* 10, no. 3 (2005): 3–21.

Atkinson, R. *Crusade: The Untold Story of the Persian Gulf War*. New York: Marinar Books, 1994.

Baker, P. "White House Scraps Bush's Approach to Missile Shield." *New York Times*, http://www.nytimes.com/2009/09/18/world/europe/18shield.html.

Balmas, M., and T. Sheafer. "Candidate Image in Election Campaigns: Attribute Agenda Setting, Affective Priming, and Voting Intentions." *International Journal of Public Opinion Research* 22, no. 2 (2010): 204–29.

Balz, D., and H. Johnson. *The Battle for America 2008: The Story of an Extraordinary Election*. New York: Viking, 2009.

Baum, M. A. "Soft news and political knowledge: Evidence of absence or absence of evidence?" *Political Communication* 20, no. 2 (2003): 173–90.

Baum, M. A. "Circling the Wagons: Soft News and Isolationism in American Public Opinion." *International Studies Quarterly* 48, no. 2 (2004a): 313–38.

Baum, M. A. "Sex, Lies, and War: How Soft News Brings Foreign Policy to the Inattentive Public." *American Political Science Review* 96, no. 1 (2004b): 91–109.

Baum, M. A. Coalition of the Unrestrained: Mass Media, Electoral Institutions and the Constraining Effect of Public Opinion Regarding Iraq. Paper presented at the 2008 Meeting of the American Political Science Association, Boston.

Baum, M. A., and A. S. Jamison. "The Oprah Effect: How Soft News Helps Inattentive Citizens Vote Consistently." *Journal of Politics* 68, no. 4 (2006): 946–59.

Baumgartner, F. R., S. De Boef, and A. E. Boydstun. *The Decline of the Death Penalty and the Discovery of Innocence*. New York: Cambridge University Press, 2008.

Baumgartner, J., and J. S. Morris. "The Daily Show Effect: Candidate Evaluations, Efficacy, and American Youth." *American Politics Research* 34, no. 3 (2006): 341–67.

Bennett, S. E., S. L. Rhine, R. S. Flickinger, and L. L. M. Bennett. "Video Malaise" Revisited: Public Trust in the Media and Government." *The Harvard International Journal of Press/Politics* 4, no. 4 (1999): 8–23.

Bennett, W. L. "Toward a Theory of Press-State Relations in the United-States." *Journal of Communication* 40, no. 2 (1990): 103–25.

Bennett, W. L. *News: The Politics of Illusion*. New York: Longman, 2002.

Bennett, W. L. "Operation Perfect Storm: The Press and the Iraq War." *Political Communication Report* 13, no. 3 (2003). http://www.opendemocracy.co.uk/content/articles/PDF/1457.pdf.

Bennett, W. L., and S. Iyengar. "A New Era of Minimal Effects? The Changing Foundations of Political Communication." *Journal of Communication* 58, no. 4 (2008): 707–31.

Bennett, W. L., R. G. Lawrence, and S. Livingston. "None Dare Call It Torture: Indexing and the Limits of Press Independence in the Abu Ghraib Scandal." *Journal of Communication* 56, no. 3 (2006): 467–85.

Bennett, W. L., R. G. Lawrence, and S. Livingston. *When the Press Fails: Political Power and the News Media from Iraq to Katrina*: University Of Chicago Press, 2007.

Bennett, W. L. and Paletz, D. L., eds. *Taken by Storm: The Media, Public Opinion, and U.S. Foreign Policy in the Gulf War*. Chicago: University of Chicago Press, 1994.

Berry, J. P. *John F. Kennedy and the Media: The First Television President*. Langam, MD: University Press of America, 1987.

Boehlert, E. *Lapdogs: How the Press Rolled over for Bush*. New York: Free Press, 2006.

Borjesson, K. *Feet to the Fire: The Media after 9/11: Top Journalists Speak Out*. Amherst, NY: Prometheus Books, 2005.

Bragg, R. *I Am a Soldier, Too: The Jessica Lynch Story*: New York: Alfred A, Knopf, 2003.

Cappella, J. N., and K. H. Jamieson. *Spiral of Cynicism: The Press and the Public Good*. New York: Oxford University Press, 1997.

Catholics in Alliance for the Common Good. "Ohio Billboard Quotes Biblical Call to Treat Immigrants with Compassion and Justice." http://www.catholicsinalliance.org/node/18476.

Celeb TV.com. "Sarah Palin: I Can See Russia from My House, Tina Fey." YouTube, http://www.youtube.com/watch?v=psyo4JDbJJ4.

Chaffee, S. H., and M. J. Metzger. "The End of Mass Communication?" *Mass Communication & Society* 4, no. 4 (2001): 365–79.

CNN staff. "Commander in Chief Lands on *USS Lincoln*." CNN.com, http://www.cnn.com/2003/ALLPOLITICS/05/01/bush.carrier.landing/.

Cottle, S. *Ethnic Minorities and the Media*. London: Open University Press, 2000.

Covert, T. Adkins, and P. C. Washburn. "Measuring Media Bias: A Content Analysis of Time and Newsweek Coverage of Domestic Social Issues, 1975–2000." *Social Science Quarterly* 88, no. 3 (2007): 690–706.

Cronkite, W. *A Reporter's Life*. New York: Random House, 1997.

D'Alessio, D., and M. Allen. "Media Bias in Presidential Elections: A Meta-Analysis." *Journal of Communication* 50, no. 4 (2000): 133–56.

Dallek, R., L. C. Gardner, T. Gittinger, D. M. Barrett, M. Beschloss, J. K. Galbraith, and A. R. Isaacs. *Flawed Giant: Lyndon Johnson and His Times, 1961–1973*. New York: Oxford University Press, 1998.

Danner, M. "Words in a Time of War: On Rhetoric, Truth and Power." Mark Danner. com, http://www.markdanner.com/articles/show/136.

Darby, J. *Northern Ireland: The Background to the Conflict*. Syracuse, NY: Syracuse University Press, 1987.

Delli Carpini, M. X. "The Inherent Arbitrariness of the 'News' Versus 'Enterntainment' Distinction." Social Science Research Council, http://publicsphere.ssrc.org/delli-car-pini-the-inherent-arbitrariness-of-the-news-versus-entertainment-distinction/.

Denton, R. *The 2008 Presidential Campaign: A Communication Perspective*: Lanham, MD: Rowman & Littlefield, 2009.

Dixon, T. L., and C. L. Azocar. "Priming Crime and Activating Blackness: Understanding the Psychological Impact of the Overrepresentation of Blacks as Lawbreakers on Television News." *Journal of Communication* 57, no. 2 (2007): 229–53.

Donaldson, G. *Liberalism's Last Hurrah: The Presidential Campaign of 1964*. Armonk, NY: M.E. Sharpe, 2003.

Dorman, W., and S. Livingston. "News and Historical Content: The Establishment Phase of the Persian Gulf Policy Debate." In W. L. Bennett and D. L. Paletz (Eds.), *Taken by Storm: The Media, Public Opinion, and U.S. Foreign Policy in the Gulf War*. Chicago: University of Chicago Press, 1994, 63–81.

Druckman, J. N. "Priming the Vote: Campaign Effects in a US Senate Election." *Political Psychology* (2004): 577–94.

Dunaway, J., R. P. Branton, and M. A. Abrajano. "Agenda Setting, Public Opinion, and the Issue of Immigration Reform." *Social Science Quarterly* 91, no. 2 (2010): 359–78.

Elliot, J. "The Ten Most Important WikiLeaks Revelations." http://www.salon.com/ news/wikileaks/?story=/political/war_room/2010/11/29/wikileaks_roundup.

El-Nawawy, M., and A. Iskander. *Al-Jazeera: How the Free Arab News Network Scooped the World and Changed the Middle East*. New York: Basic Books, 2002.

Entman, R. A. "Framing US Coverage of International News: Contrasts in Narratives of the Kal and Iran Air Incidents." *Journal of Communication* 41, no. 4 (1991): 6–27.

Entman, R. M. *Projections of Power: Framing News, Public Opinion, and US Foreign Policy*. Chicago: University of Chicago Press, 2004.

Entman, R. M. "Blacks in the News: Television, Modern Racism, and Cultural Change." In A. Reynolds and B. Barnett (Eds.), *Communication and Law: Multidisciplinary Approaches to Research*. New York: Routledge, 2006, 205–26.

Entman, R. M., and A. Rojecki. *The Black Image in the White Mind: Media and Race in America*. Chicago: University of Chicago Press, 2001.

Esfandiari, G. "The Twitter Devolution." *Foreign Policy*, http://www.foreignpolicy.com/ articles/2010/06/07/the_twitter_revolution_that_wasnt.

Fahmy, S., and T. J. Johnson. "Show the Truth and Let Al Jazeera Audience Decide: Support for Use of Graphic Imagery among Al Jazeera Viewers." *Journal of Broadcasting & Electronic Media*, 51, no. 2 (2007): 245–64.

Fairness and Accuracy in Reporting. "Examining The 'Liberal Media' Claim." Fairness and Accuracy in Reporting, http://www.fair.org/index.php?page=2447.

Farrell, J. "A Noun, a Verb and 9/11." *Concord Monitor*, http://www.concordmonitor. com/article/noun-verb-and-911.

Fay, M. T., M. Morrissey, and M. Smyth. *Northern Ireland's Troubles: The Human Costs*. London: Pluto Press, 1999.

Finnegan, L. *No Questions Asked: News Coverage since 9/11*. Westport, CT: Praeger, 2006.

Fokenflik, D.. "Building Bipartisanship? Not Limbaugh's Problem." National Public Radio, http://www.npr.org/templates/story/story.php?storyId=7018083.

Fox News. "Intel Used by Obama Found Iran Long-Range Missile Capacity Would Take 3-5 Years Longer." http://www.foxnews.com/politics/2009/09/18/intel-used-obama-iran-long-range-missile-capacity-years-longe.

Gamson, W. A. *Talking Politics*. New York: Cambridge University Press, 1992.

Gamson, W. A., and Modigliani, A. Media Discourse and Public Opinion on Nuclear Power: A Constructionist Approach." *American Journal of Sociology* 95, no. 1 (1989): 1–37.

Gannett Foundation Media Center. *The Media at War: The Press and the Persian Gulf Conflict*. New York: Columbia University Press, 1991.

Garver, E. *Aristotle's Rhetoric: An Art of Character* Chicago: University of Chicago Press, 1994.

Geer, J. G. "Fanning the Flames: The News Media's Role in the Rise of Negativity in Presidential Campaigns." *Discussion Paper Series*: Joan Shorenstein Center on the Press, Politics, and Public Policy, Harvard University, February, 2010.

Gerbner, G., and L. Gross. "Living with Television: The Violence Profile." *Journal of Communication* 26, no. 2 (1976): 172–94.

Goldberg, B. "Bias: A CBS Insider Exposes How the Media Distort the News." *Journalism Studies* 4, no. 2 (2003): 287–94.

Goldman, P., T. M., DeFrank, M. Miller, A. Murr, and T. Matthews. *Quest for the Presidency 1992*. College Station, Texas: Texas A&M Press, 1994.

Goldstein, K., and T. N. Ridout. "Measuring the Effects of Televised Political Advertising in the United States." *Annual Review of Political Science* 7 (2004): 205–26.

Groseclose, T., and J. Milyo. "A Measure of Media Bias." *The Quarterly Journal of Economics* 120, no. 4 (2005): 1191–237.

Halberstram, D. *The Powers That Be*. New York: Alfred A. Knopf, 1979.

Hallin, D. C. *The Uncensored War: The Media and Vietnam*. Berkeley: University of California Press, 1989.

Hammond, W. M. *Reporting Vietnam: Media and Military at War*. Lawrence: University Press of Kansas, 1998.

Harris, J. F. *The Survivor: Bill Clinton in the White House*. New York: Random House, 2006.

Healy, P. "Clinton Gives War Critics New Answer on '02 Vote." http://www.nytimes.com/2007/02/18/us/politics/18clinton.html.

Heilemann, J., and M. Halperin. *Game Change: Obama and the Clintons, Mccain and Palin, and the Race of a Lifetime*. New York: Harper, 2010.

Hersh, S. *Chain of Command: The Road from 9/11 to Abu Ghraib*. New York: HarperCollins, 2004.

Hertsgaard, M. *On Bended Knee: The Press and the Reagan Presidency*. New York: Schocken, 1989.

Hetherington, M. "Declining Trust and a Shrinking Policy Agenda: Why the Media Scholars Should Care." In Roderick P. Hart and Daron Shaw (Eds.), *Communication in US Elections: New Agendas*. New York: Rowman and Littlefield, 2001, 105–21.

Huber, G. A., and K. Arceneaux. "Identifying the Persuasive Effects of Presidential Advertising." *American Journal of Political Science* 51, no. 4 (2007): 957–77.

Hume, E., and V. Reform. "Talk Show Culture." In D. H. (Ed.), *Encyclopedia of International Media and Communications,* (Vol. 4), 2003, http://www.ellenhume.com/articles/talkshow_printable.htm#overview.

INDenverTimes. "Boulder Police Will Be Scrutinizing Naked Bicyclists in Saturday Protest." INDenverTimes, http://www.indenvertimes.com/boulder-police-will-be-scrutinizing-naked-bicyclists-in-saturday-protest/comment-page-1/.

Israeli Ministry for Foreign Affairs. "More Israelis Have Been Killed by Palestinian Terrorists since Oslo." Israeli Ministry for Foreign Affairs, http://www.mfa.gov.il/MFA/MFAArchive/1990_1999/1998/9/More%20Israelis%20Have%20Been%20Killed%.

Iyengar, S. *Is Anyone Responsible?: How Television Frames Political Issues*. Chicago: University of Chicago Press, 1994.

Iyengar, S., and D. R. Kinder. *News That Matters: Television and American Opinion*. Chicago: University of Chicago Press, 1988.

Jasperson, A. E., and M. O. El-Kikhia. "CNN and Al-Jazeera's Media Coverage of America's War in Afghanistan." In P. Norris, M. Kern, and M. Just (Eds.), *Framing Terrorism: The News Media, the Government, and the Public*. New York: Routledge, 2003, 113–32.

Johnson, T. J., and S. Fahmy. "The CNN of the Arab World or a Shill for Terrorists?: How Support for Press Freedom and Political Ideology Predict Credibility of Al-Jazeera among Its Audience." *International Communication Gazette* 70, no. 5 (2008): 338–60.

Kagan, K. *The Surge: A Military History*. New York: Encounter Books, 2008.

Kaid, L. L., and M. Postelnicu. "Political Advertising in the 2004 Election: Comparison of Traditional Television and Internet Messages." *American Behavioral Scientist* 49, no. 2 (2005): 265–78.

Kampfner, J. "The Truth About Jessica." *The Guardian* 15 (2003).

Kirk, R. *The Conservative Mind: From Burke to Eliot*. Washington, DC: Regnery Press, 2001.

Klein, A. J. *Striking Back: The 1972 Munich Olympics Massacre and Israel's Deadly Response*. New York: Random House, 2007.

Kohut, A. "Cable and Internet Loom Large in Fragmented Political News Universe." http://www.pewinternet.org/Reports/2004/Cable-and-Internet-Loom-Large-in-Fragmented-Political-News-Universe.

Komonews. "Naked Bicyclists Ride in Protest over Environmental Abuse." Komonews.com, http://www.komonews.com/news/archive/4126851.html.

Krosnick, J. A., and L. A. Brannon. "The Impact of the Gulf War on the Ingredients of Presidential Evaluations: Multidimensional Effects of Political Involvement." *American Political Science Review* (1993): 963–75.

Krugman, P. *The Conscience of a Liberal*. New York: W. W. Norton, 2007.

Kull, S., C. Ramsay, and E. Lewis. "Misperceptions, the Media, and the Iraq War." *Political Science Quarterly* 118, no. 4 (2003): 569–98.

Laser, M. "Ralph Nader: Internet Not So Hot At 'Motivating Action'." http://arstechnica.com/web/news/2009/05/ralph-nader-internet-not-so-hot-at-motivating-action.ars.

Lawrence, R. G. *The Politics of Force: Media and the Construction of Police Brutality*. Berkeley: University of California Press, 2000.

Lawrence, E., J. Sides, and H. Farrell. "Self-segregation or deliberation? Blog readership, participation, and polarization in American politics." *Perspectives on Politics* 8, no. 1 (2004): 141–157.

Lee, M. A., and N. Solomon. *Unreliable Sources: A Guide to Detecting Bias in News Media*. New York: Lyle Stuart, 1991.

Leskovec, J., L. Backstrom, and J. Kleinberg. "Meme-Tracking and the Dynamics of the News Cycle." Paper presented at the 15th International Conference on Knowledge Discovery and Data Mining, Paris, France 2009.

Lewis, J. *Shoot First and Ask Questions Later: Media Coverage of the 2003 Iraq War*. New York: Peter Lang, 2006.

Lichter, S. R., S. Rothman, and L. S. Lichter. *The Media Elite: America's New Powerbrokers*. New York: Hastings House, 1990.

Limbaugh, R. "Rush the Vote: Operation Chaos Meeting and Exceeding Objectives." http://www.rushlimbaugh.com/home/daily/site_031908/content/01125108.guest. html.

Livingston, S., and D. A. Van Belle. "The Effects of Satellite Technology on Newsgathering from Remote Locations." *Political Communication* 22, no. 1 (2005): 45–62.

Livingston, S., and W. L. Bennett. "Gatekeeping, Indexing, and Live-Event News: Is Technology Altering the Construction of News?" *Political Communication* 20, no. 4 (2003): 363–80.

Lukacs, Y. *Israel, Jordan, and the Peace Process*. Syracuse, NY: Syracuse University Press, 1999.

Lynch, M. *Voices of the New Arab Public: Iraq, Al-Jazeera, and Middle East Politics Today*. New York: Columbia University Press, 2006.

MacArthur, J. R. *Second Front: Censorship and Propaganda in the 1991 Gulf War*. Berkeley: University of California Press, 2004.

Malcom, A. "Barak Obama Wants to Be President of These 57 States." http://latimes-blogs.latimes.com/washington/2008/05/barack-obama-wa.html.

Matthews, J. J. "To Defeat a Maverick: The Goldwater Candidacy Revisited, 1963–1964." *Presidential Studies Quarterly* 27, no. 4 (1997).

May, A. L. "Swift Boat Vets in 2004: Press Coverage of an Independent Campaign." *First Amendment Law Review,* 4 (2005): 66.

Mazzetti, M., J. Perlez, E. Schmitt, and A. W. Lehren. "Pakistan Aids Insurgency in Afghanistan, Reports Assert." http://www.nytimes.com/2010/07/26/world/asia/26isi. html?_r=1.

McCombs, M. "A Look at Agenda-Setting: Past, Present and Future." *Journalism Studies* 6, no. 4 (2005): 543–57.

McCombs, M. E., and D. L. Shaw. "The Agenda-Setting Function of Mass Media." *Public Opinion Quarterly* 36, no. 2 (1972): 176–87.

McGarry, J., and B. O'Leary. *The Northern Ireland Conflict: Consociational Engagements*. New York: Oxford University Press, 2004.

Mermin, J. *Debating War and Peace: Media Coverage of US Intervention in the Post-Vietnam Era*. Princeton, NJ: Princeton University Press, 1999.

Miles, H. Al-Jazeera: The Inside Story of the Arab News Channel That Is Challenging the West. New York: Grove Press, 2005.

Mills, D. "Attack of the Giant Negroes!!" Undercover Black Man, http://undercover-blackman.blogspot.com/2007/07/attack-of-giant-negroes.html.

Mitchell, G. J. *Making Peace*. Berkeley: University of California Press, 2000.

Morgan, M., and J. Shanahan. "Two Decades of Cultivation Analysis: An Appraisal and Meta-Analysis." *Communication Yearbook 20* (1997): 1–45.

Morozov, E. "From Slacktivism to Activism." Foreign Policy, http://neteffect.foreignpolicy.com/posts/2009/09/05/from_slacktivism_to_activism.

Moy, P., and D. A. Scheufele. "Media Effects on Political and Social Trust." *Journalism and Mass Communication Quarterly* 77, no. 4 (2000): 744–59.

Moy, P., M. A. Xenos, and V. K. Hess. "Priming Effects of Late-Night Comedy." *International Journal of Public Opinion Research* 18, no. 2 (2006): 198–210.

Muller, L., and B. Wuest. Media Malaise or Mobilization: How Mass Media Affect Electoral Participation in Established Democracies. Paper presented at the *5th ECPR Conference*. Postdam, Germany, 2009.

Nasaw, D. *The Chief: The Life of William Randolph Hears*. Boston: Mariner Books, 2001.

National Commission on Terrorist Attacks Upon the United States. "Al Qaeda Aims at the American Homeland." U.S. Government Printing Office, http://govinfo.library. unt.edu/911/report/911Report_Ch5.pdf.

National Highway Traffic Safety Administration. "Fatal Crashes 1994–2008." http:// www-fars.nhtsa.dot.gov/Trends/TrendsGeneral.aspx.

National Organization for Women. "Reproductive Justice Is Every Woman's Right." National Organization of Women, http://www.now.org/issues/abortion/reproductive_justice.html.

National Right to Life. "Abortion: Medical Facts." National Right to Life, http://www. nrlc.org/abortion/index.html.

Nelson, T. E., R. A. Clawson, and Z. M. Oxley. "Media Framing of a Civil Liberties Conflict and Its Effect on Tolerance." *American Political Science Review* 91 (1997): 567–84.

Niven, D. *Tilt?: The Search for Media Bias*. Westport, CT: Praeger, 2002.

Norris, P. *A Virtuous Circle: Political Communications in Postindustrial Societies*. New York: Cambridge University Press, 2000.

Novack, R. "Immigration and Terrorism." Townhall.com, http://townhall.com/ columnists/RobertNovak/2006/07/06/immigration_and_terrorism.

Paterson, C. "News Agency Dominance in International News on the Internet." In D. Skinner, J. R. Compton, and M. Gasher (Eds.), *Converging Media, Diverging Interests: A Political Economy of News in the United States and Canada,* Lantham, MA: Lexington Books, 2005, 33–49.

Patterson, T. E. *The Vanishing Voter*. New York: Vintage Books, 2003.

Patterson, T. E., and W. Donsbach. "News Decisions: Journalists as Partisan Actors." *Political Communication* 13, no. 4 (1996): 455–68.

Peri, Y. *The Assassination of Yitzhak Rabin*. Stanford, CA: Stanford University Press, 2000.

Petri, A. "Refudiate: Sarah Palin's New Political Language." *Washington Post*, http://voices. washingtonpost.com/postpartisan/2010/07/refudiate_sarah_palins_new_pol.html.

Pew Internet and American Life Project. "The New News Landscape: Rise of the Internet." http://pewresearch.org/pubs/1508/internet-cell-phone-users-news-social-experience.

Pew Project for Excellence in Journalism. "The State of the News Media: An Annual Report on American Journalism." Pew Research Center for People & the Press http:// www.stateofthemedia.org/2010/online_audience.php#whoareonline.

Pew Research Center for the People & the Press. "Two-in-Three Critical of Bush's Relief Efforts." Pew Research Center, http://people-press.org/report/255/two-in-three-critical-of-bushs-relief-efforts.

Pew Research Center for the People & the Press. "Partisanship and Cable News Audiences." Pew Research Center Publications, http://pewresearch.org/pubs/1395/ partisanship-fox-news-and--other-cable-news-audiences.

Pew Research Center for the People & the Press. "Most Voters Say News Media Wants Obama to Win." Pew Research Center for the People & the Press, http://pewresearch. org/pubs/1003/joe-the-plumber.

Pew Research Center's Project for Excellence in Journalism. "How the Press Reported the 2008 General Election." Pew Research Center for The People & the Press, http:// www.journalism.org/node/13307.

Priest, D., and W. M. Arkin. "A Hidden World, Growing Beyond Control." http:// projects.washingtonpost.com/top-secret-america/articles/a-hidden-world-growing-beyond-control/.

Prior, M. "News Vs. Entertainment: How Increasing Media Choice Widens Gaps in Political Knowledge and Turnout." *American Journal of Political Science* 49, no. 3 (2005): 577–92.

Procter, B. H. *William Randolph Hearst: The Early Years, 1863–1910.* New York: Oxford University Press, 1998.

Putnam, R. D. *Bowling Alone: The Collapse and Revival of American Community.* New York: Simon and Schuster, 2001.

Quattrone, G. A., and Tversky, A. "Rational and Psychological Analyses of Political Choice." *The American Political Science Review* 82, no. 3 (1988): 719–36.

Reeve, S. *One Day in September: The Full Story of the 1972 Munich Olympics Massacre and the Israeli Revenge Operation "Wrath of God."* New York: Arcade Publishing, 2000.

Reuters. "Timeline: Attacks on U.S. Targets." Reuters, http://www.reuters.com/article/idUSTRE6411QA20100502.

Roberts, G., and H. Klibanoff. *The Race Beat: The Press, the Civil Rights Struggle, and the Awakening of a Nation.* New York: Alfred A. Knopf, 2006.

Robinson, M. J. "Public Affairs Television and the Growth of Political Malaise: The Case Of 'The Selling of the Pentagon'." *The American Political Science Review* 70, no. 2 (1976): 409–32.

Romer, D., K. H. Jamieson, and S. Aday. "Television News and the Cultivation of Fear of Crime." *Journal of Communication* 53, no. 1 (2003): 88–104.

Ruane, J., and J. Todd. *The Dynamics of Conflict in Northern Ireland: Power, Conflict, and Emancipation.* New York: Cambridge University Press, 1996.

Runkel, D. R. *Campaign for President: The Managers Look at '88.* Dover, MA: Auburn House, 1989.

Schectman, J. "Iran's Twitter Revolution? Maybe Not Yet." Bloomberg.com, http://www.businessweek.com/technology/content/jun2009/tc20090617_803990.htm.

Schudson, M. "A Family of Public Spheres." Social Science Research Council, http://publicsphere.ssrc.org/schudson-a-family-of-public-spheres/.

Seelye, K. Q. "Clinton Bowls over Media." *New York Times*, http://thecaucus.blogs.nytimes.com/2008/04/02/clinton-bowls-over-media./

Sheafer, T. "How to Evaluate It: The Role of Story-Evaluative Tone in Agenda Setting and Priming." *Journal of Communication* 57, no. 1 (2007): 21–39.

Sheafer, T., and I. Gabay. "Mediated Public Diplomacy: A Strategic Contest over International Agenda Building and Frame Building." *Political Communication* 26, no. 4 (2009): 447–67.

Sheafer, T., and G. Weimann. "Agenda Building, Agenda Setting, Priming, Individual Voting Intentions, and the Aggregate Results: An Analysis of Four Israeli Elections." *The Journal of Communication* 55, no. 2 (2005): 347–65.

Sprinzak, E. *Brother against Brother: Violence and Extremism in Israeli Politics from Altalena to the Rabin Assassination.* New York: Free Press, 1999.

Stohl, M. "Old Myths, New Fantasies and the Enduring Realities of Terrorism." *Critical Studies in Terrorism* 1, no. 1 (2008): 5–16.

Thomas, E. "The Myth of Objectivity." *Newsweek*, March 1, 2008, 43–44.

Tucker, B., and P. L. Walton. "From General's Daughter to Coal Miner's Daughter: Spinning and Counter-Spinning Jessica Lynch." *Canadian Review of American Studies* 36, no. 3 (2006): 311–30.

Tumber, H., and J. Palmer. *Media at War: The Iraq Crisis.* Thousand Oaks, CA Sage, 2004.

Tversky, A., and D. Kahneman. "The Framing of Decisions and the Psychology of Choice." *Science* 211, no. 4481 (1981): 453–58.

Tyndall Report. "Tydnall Report 2009 in Review." http://tyndallreport.com/yearinreview2009.

Valentino, N. A., M. N. Beckmann, and T. A. Buhr. "A Spiral of Cynicism for Some: The Contingent Effects of Campaign News Frames on Participation and Confidence in Government." *Political Communication* 18, no. 4 (2001): 347–67.

Valentino, N. A., V. L. Hutchings, and D. Williams. "The Impact of Political Advertising on Knowledge, Internet Information Seeking, and Candidate Preference." *Journal of Communication* 54, no. 2 (2004): 337–54.

Van Dijk, T. A. "New (S) Racism: A Discourse Analytical Approach." In S. Cottle. (Ed.), *Ethnic Minorities and the Media*. London: Open University Press, 2000, 33–49.

Van Noije, L., J. Kleinnijenhuis, and D. Oegema, "Loss of Parliamentary Control Due to Mediatization and Europeanization: A Longitudinal and Cross-Sectional Analysis of Agenda Building in the United Kingdom and the Netherlands," *British Journal of Political Science* 38, no. 3 (2008), 455–78.

Viswanath, K. and J. R. Finnegan, "The Knowledge Gap Hypothesis: Twenty-Five Years Later," *Communication Yearbook 19,* Thousand Oaks, CA: Sage, 1996, 187–227

Wanta, W., G. Golan, and C. Lee, "Agenda Setting and International News: Media Influence on Public Perceptions of Foreign Nations." *Journalism and Mass Communication Quartlerly* 81, no. 2 (2004), 364–67.

Wanta, W., and Y. Kalyango Jr, "Terrorism and Africa: A Study of Agenda Building in the United States." *International Journal of Public Opinion Research* 19, no. 4 (2007), 435–50.

Weinmann, G., *Terror on the Internet: The New Arena, the New Challenges*. Washington, D.C.: The United States Institute of Peace, 2006.

Washington Times Staff. "Editorial: Iran's Twitter Revolution." http://www.washingtontimes.com/news/2009/jun/16/irans-twitter-revolution/.

White, T. H. *The Making of the President, 1964*. New York: Signet, 1965.

Wolfsfeld, G. *Media and Political Conflict: News from the Middle East*. New York: Cambridge University Press, 1997.

Wolfsfeld, G. *Media and the Path to Peace*. New York: Cambridge University Press, 2004.

Wolfsfeld, G., E. Y. Alimi, and W. Kailani. "News Media and Peace Building in Asymmetrical Conflicts: The Flow of News between Jordan and Israel." *Political Studies* 56, no. 2 (2008): 374–98.

Wyatt, C. R. *Paper Soldiers*. Chicago: University of Chicago Press.

Zaller, J. *The Nature and Origins of Mass Opinion*. New York: Cambridge University Press, 1992.

Zaller, J. "The Myth of Massive Media Impact Revived: New Support for a Discredited Idea." In Diana Carole Mutz, Paul M. Sniderman, and Richard A. Brody (Eds.), *Political Persuasion and Attitude Change*. Ann Arbor, University of Michigan Press, 1996, 17–78.

Zayani, M. *The Al Jazeera Phenomenon: Critical Perspectives on New Arab Media*. London: Paradigm, 2005.

Index